WELCOME TO MY WORLD

A STRATEGY GUIDE FOR NEW TEACHERS

WITHDRAWN

Chris Boone Cleveland

ScarecrowEducation
Lanham, Maryland • Toronto • Oxford
2004

Published in the United States of America
by ScarecrowEducation
An imprint of The Rowman & Littlefield Publishing Group, Inc.
4501 Forbes Boulevard, Suite 200, Lanham, Maryland 20706
www.scaroweducation.com

PO Box 317
Oxford
OX2 9RU, UK

British Library Cataloguing in Publication Information Available

Library of Congress Cataloging-in-Publication Data

Cleveland, Chris Boone, 1960–
  Welcome to my world : a strategy guide for new teachers /
Chris Boone Cleveland.
      p. cm.
  ISBN 1-57886-150-0 (pbk. : alk. paper)
  1. First year teachers. I. Title.
LB2844.1.N4C58 2004
371.1—dc22

                                    2004002912

∞™ The paper used in this publication meets the minimum requirements of
American National Standard for Information Sciences—Permanence of Paper
for Printed Library Materials, ANSI/NISO Z39.48-1992.
Manufactured in the United States of America.

To my dad, Bill Boone, who began teaching in 1960, the same year that I was born. After forty years, he retired from teaching in the public schools, but he still teaches me every day by the example that he sets with his life. Thank you, Dad, for always believing in me, even when I didn't believe in myself.

CONTENTS

ACKNOWLEDGMENTS

From the first day I stepped into a classroom as a teacher, I knew I had found my niche in life. Often during the past twenty years, I have felt as though my students have taught me almost as much as I have taught them. Almost every day is filled with new ideas and new experiences. My hope is that this book will help new teachers as they pursue what I believe is the greatest and most rewarding career a person could choose.

I would like to thank all of the teachers who gave me their stories, poems, ideas, and experiences and allowed me to share them with the readers of this book. Most of these teachers have asked to remain nameless, but all of the narratives in this book are from them.

I would also like to thank my husband, Keith, for the many hours of reading and rereading that he did, for the many suggestions that he gave, and for reassuring me that I was making a difference in the lives of my students on those days when I felt like everything was going wrong.

Finally, I would like to thank Mr. Steve Welchans, who was my freshmen biology and advanced biology teacher. He was the teacher that I wanted to be like, the one who inspired me to be a teacher by his actions and attitudes in the classroom. He is still teaching today at Fountain Central High School in Veedersburg, Indiana, and I'm sure he is still inspiring his students to achieve at the highest level that they can, in every aspect of their lives.

1

WELCOME TO
MY WORLD

So, You've Decided to Be a Teacher?

Being a new teacher is rather like becoming a new parent. You take the classes, prepare yourself for your new life, and then suddenly you realize that you're not sure what to expect. Panic may set in during the weeks before the first day of school as you begin to consider all the horror stories that well-meaning people have told you about education today. Relax, take deep breaths, and concentrate on why you decided to become a teacher in the first place.

Chances are you decided to become a teacher because somewhere along the way a teacher made an impression on you. Who was your favorite teacher? What qualities did he or she have that impressed you? Amazingly, you will find that it was not the teacher who gave the easy A, who showed the most movies, or who wanted everyone to see him or her as a friend. Chances are that your favorite teacher is the one who inspired you to do your best work, the one you never wanted to disappoint by not having your work done, the one who took classroom teaching seriously, and the one who believed that a grade meant something. Remember those qualities. They are the ones *you* will want to develop in your teaching career.

Becoming a teacher is not a process that ends when you complete your degree and accept your first teaching position; it is a continual process. The best teachers learn something new every single day. This is what makes them great teachers: a desire to learn and a desire to open the minds of students to the rewards that knowledge can provide.

UNREALISTIC EXPECTATIONS

Teachers are, in a way, dreamers. They dream about students who are always prepared for class and listen attentively because they love to learn. They dream about environments where education is the number one priority and communities where parents and school boards are supportive of a teacher's policies and excellence is not just a word on a mission statement. In other words, they dream about life in Mayberry not Boston Public. How many episodes do you suppose there were on *The Andy Griffith Show* that revolved around Opie and school? Opie rarely got a break; Andy was always on the side of Opie's teacher, and Opie usually learned an important lesson about life.

Keep believing in Mayberry. You can create an atmosphere of learning and respect in your classroom. Don't let others dictate your philosophy and tell you that your expectations are unrealistic. Will it be easy? No. Will it get easier? Yes.

Many teachers today have, unfortunately, accepted society's view of education. We are living in a society that seems to have lost a great deal of respect for teachers and education. Much of this can be traced to societal issues too complex and lengthy to be discussed here, and some of it can be traced to teachers who have quit fighting for what they know is right. As a teacher, you cannot change the minds of society, a community, or even one school, but you can change the minds of your students and their parents. Do not get bogged down trying to solve all the problems of education. Stay focused on your "little corner of the world." Your expectations of a classroom where learning is the number one priority are not unrealistic; they are admirable. Hang on to those expectations!

WHAT'S YOUR TYPE?

When deciding what type of teacher you want to be, it is helpful to first focus on the traits that a successful teacher possesses. The five qualities listed in this section are not the only ones a teacher needs, but they are certainly a step in the right direction. Each is followed by a quotation that represents it and then an interpretation of how this can be applied to the classroom. The author of each of these quotations is Texas Tech Coach Bob Knight, a man whose commitment to education has been well documented. These quotations deserve to be studied carefully by teachers who want to make a lasting impression on their students.

Preparation, Prevention, Patience, Perseverance, and Push: The Qualities Necessary to Successfully Educate Young People

1. Preparation

   "A coach must remember that he is a teacher and therefore must prepare his team for every possible situation that may develop." As a teacher, your job is to prepare your students for a wide variety of situations, not just a select few. You are also responsible for varying your instruction to meet the needs of different types of students. Not only do you need to prepare your students, a quality teacher also is prepared to meet the changing demands of her classes.

2. Prevention

   "The best teachers I've known are intolerant people. They don't tolerate mistakes." There is a difference between accepting mistakes and tolerating them, and a wise teacher soon learns which of the two will benefit students. Students must have the freedom to learn from their mistakes and a desire not to repeat them.

3. Patience

   "Coaching is a great balance between demand and patience. The coaches who are demanding—constantly demanding—are not particularly good coaches. There's a balance between the two that I think is really important. Patience allows for development; demand brings about development at a rate that you have to have." Your students need to feel that their education is important to you and that you have set goals for them, goals that will make them successful. You must be willing to do everything you can to help them reach the goals that they have set for themselves as well as the goals that you have set for them.

4. Perseverance

"The coach that really coaches and really teaches is the guy who goes out on a limb, even though some kid isn't going to like him, or the team isn't going to like him. But he's out there doing that because it's the best way to get kids to play as well as they can." You must be prepared to accept that sometimes others are not going to appreciate your dedication. Keep your eyes on the goal. Do not give up on your students. Once they realize how important their education is to you, they will respond by doing their best in your class.

5. Push

"In leadership, you're trying to get people to be better than they think they can be, to reach within themselves. You're trying to get a guy to do something he doesn't want to do—and do it well." Students do not have to love your class; they have to learn from your class. It is your job to inspire them to want to learn. Remind your students often that they have the potential to be great thinkers and great doers. Nothing is more inspirational to students than a teacher's confidence in their abilities.

Bob Knight has sometimes been a controversial figure. Some people think he is the greatest coach to ever step onto the hardwood, while others question his tactics. Few, however, can argue with his tremendous results and accomplishments. At times you, too, may be misunderstood, but you will also experience moments as a teacher that you will cherish—moments when you realize that you have made a significant impact on a student's life. Choosing to excel in teaching is not easy, but the rewards are there. Teachers have never been needed in our society as much as they are needed today, and your choice to become a teacher is one that should be commended.

BUILT WITH YOU IN MIND

The teaching shortage in America is reaching critical stages. Many schools and state governments are offering cash incentives, tempting benefits, and other perks in order to coax our nation's youth into teaching in their corporations. Yet, many young teachers are still leaving the field of education after only a year or two. Why? How can these young people walk away from a career that many of them had planned to pursue since they were in junior high? The main problem seems to be that new teachers are not completely prepared for the realities of teaching. New teachers need to have a realistic idea of what to expect when they enter the classroom for the first time. They need to be given honest advice and concrete ideas. They also need to know how to go about achieving the goals and dreams that they have for their students. Most importantly, they need to have a strategy, a plan for developing a classroom atmosphere that will benefit both teacher and students. A teacher armed with a definite strategy for educating her students and a desire to give them the best education possible will be a teacher that will make a difference in the lives of countless students.

Without a strategy in mind, a new teacher may feel overwhelmed. Although many school corporations have excellent new teacher training programs and some states have mentoring programs for first-year teachers, eventually, a teacher is ultimately alone in a classroom, confronted with an idea that may be as terrifying as it is exciting—she is in charge. Throughout this book you will find several methods and ideas that have been successfully used in the classroom. *Welcome to My World* was, indeed, built with you in mind. This strategy guide can help new teachers get started on the right path to successfully educating young people. In addition, veteran teachers whose desire to excel has been somewhat thwarted by the realities of teaching will hopefully find some answers in this book as to where and why their enthusiasm has dwindled and will remember how important their initial goal was. Quality teachers are needed today—teachers who will light a fire in the world of education, a fire that encompasses students, teachers, and all those who believe that a quality education is an inherent right in a free society.

Teaching is still one of the most fulfilling and rewarding careers that an individual can choose, and despite what the media wants the public to believe, most of our school systems are in excellent shape. Although many people will argue and say that students, administrators, politicians, other teachers, and even parents have contributed to the demise of the quality in education, statistics prove otherwise. A student in the public or private school corporations can receive a much higher quality of education than students of previous generations. Computers and advanced technology have brought a type of global knowledge to today's students that previous generations could never have imagined. Another myth that seems to follow education is that teachers' salaries have not kept pace with other professional salaries. Since 1960, the average teacher's salary has increased dramatically. A teacher in 1960 earned an average salary of $4,000. The average teacher's salary in the United States in the year 2000 was $30,000, almost a 650 percent increase.

Why, then, does there seem to be such a negative attitude toward our public schools and our teachers? Part of this has to do with global competition. Our world is shrinking dramatically and competition between countries has never been greater. When the public hears that Japanese students score higher than their American counterparts on math exams, we panic. When statements are made concerning the hours that Chinese students spend studying, we can't help feeling like a nation of slackers. Americans often seem to focus on the negative rather than the positive. This attitude, which has been advanced largely by the media and politicians, has made us a nation that believes the education system has failed, and this attitude has been transmitted to our teachers and to our students. The self-fulfilling prophecy strikes again.

America's schools do not need more statewide or national tests; they do not need more money thrown at education; they do not need stricter standards. An educational fire could sweep through America using only three things: teachers who love to teach and cannot wait to share their knowledge with their students, parents who support and encourage those teachers who have made this commitment, and students who buy into the philosophy that a strong education will open any door that they may choose.

"Welcome to my world. Won't you come on in?

Miracles, I guess, still happen now and then."

Your first real challenge as a teacher starts now. Believe in miracles. Believe that you can change "your little corner of the world." The challenge is there, the rewards are there, other teachers are there, and the need for someone like you is definitely there. Today's students are, indeed, waiting just for you.

2

HELLO, WALLS

Environment Is Everything

After you accepted your teaching job, the principal probably walked you to the room assigned to you so that you could look around. As you stared at the blank walls, rows of desks, and empty shelves, you probably wondered exactly how this room could reflect your teaching style. The room that you create is important, not only to you (after all you will be spending eight hours a day here), but also to those who enter every day. The first impression that many will have of you and of your effectiveness as a teacher will come from the first glimpse they get of the environment in which you expect your students to learn.

FIRST IMPRESSIONS

Let's start with the door to your classroom. Most doors have the room number and the type of class that is taught there; many doors will also have the teacher's name listed on the outside. If yours does not, and the room is yours alone, feel free to make your own name sign by going on the computer and finding an appropriate quotation that expresses your personality. Have the sign laminated and placed on your door.

CLOSE THE DOOR ON EDUCATION

The best way to let others know your class is in session is to shut your door when the bell rings or when class time has begun. Not only will this discourage visitors from wandering in, but your students will also find it much easier to concentrate if they are not distracted by activities outside your classroom. Cultivate the habit of shutting the door at the exact time class starts every hour. Better yet, assign a student this job every day. Students actually enjoy having a job assigned to them that they are responsible for on a daily basis, no matter what age or learning level they may be. Closing the door may sound like a small detail, but the small details that run your classroom will all add up to a more productive environment for you and your students.

DO NOT DISTURB

One thing you will quickly realize after you begin teaching is that you may be interrupted frequently. Other people (teacher's aides, office workers, students, even other teachers) may come to your room during class time in order to ask you or your students questions. Sometimes, these people do not even seem to realize that they are interrupting. Set the tone early that you prefer not to be interrupted during class time. You can do this in a variety of ways. The easiest way is to smile at the person and say politely but firmly, "Could you please come back at the end of class time? We are busy at the moment."

Some teachers take this to the extreme. They are so unapproachable that an office aide is afraid to knock on the door with a pass for a student who needs to go to the office because of an emergency. You do not need to stand at the door and growl at an innocent aide. Consistency is the key. If you show others that you prefer not to be interrupted, word will soon get around that you prefer visitors to wait until class is almost finished. If this doesn't seem to be working for you, then you can always try the more direct approach—a sign.

Mr. Bill Boone, who taught school for forty-two years, had a sign on his door that read: "Teaching is the most important thing I do. Do not interrupt my students' learning unless it is an emergency." His words are simple, to the point, and easily understood. Posting a sign like this on your door or quickly letting others know by your attitude that you do not appreciate being interrupted usually works.

Why is closing your door and expecting others to value your wishes about interrupting class so important? This sends a clear message to your students that you feel strongly about what you are doing, that you value the time they spend in your classroom, and in essence, that they are the most important part of your day. You are telling them by your actions that nothing is more important to you than their education.

THE BEST SEAT IN THE HOUSE

Desk arrangement is another important detail. On that first day, as you glanced around the room at the five or six rows of approximately five desks per row, you may have felt that at least there was something that you remember from high school as being normal. Think differently. In the traditional setting, someone will always be sitting in the back and someone will always be sitting in the front. Students come in all shapes and sizes, and many of your students' views may be totally obstructed in this type of seating arrangement. Here are two nontraditional seating arrangements that you may want to try.

Desk arrangement one is an excellent choice for the teacher who is not tied to the lectern. This arrangement allows the teacher easy access to all students and provides for substantial interaction between the students and the teacher. Most teachers find that they end up walking in the walkway in the middle. Every student can be seen easily and every student can see the teacher. Students don't feel as closed in as they do in rows of four or five

Figure 2.1. Desk Arrangement One: X = One Student Desk

X	X	X		X	X	X
X	X	X		X	X	X
X	X	X		X	X	X
X	X	X		X	X	X
X	X	X		X	X	X
	Teacher's Desk		Lectern			

desks. The room will have more energy, and the teacher can easily see her students' responses and reactions. When students are working on something at their desks, this seating arrangement also allows the teacher to move easily among her students, helping them individually. If space is a problem, the same arrangement can work in an L-shape.

Another arrangement that works well is the arrangement below.

Desk Arrangement Two: X = One Student Desk

Teacher's Desk   Lectern

Figure 2.2.

This arrangement is the one that many classes will like the best. Students usually like at least one of three things about this arrangement. First of all, many of them feel it looks like a college classroom, and they immediately feel "smarter." Students also agree that this style of seating initiates better class discussion, making them feel as though the group values their opinion. Finally, some say that it shows that the teacher trusts them to sit close together. Everyone has an unobstructed view of the board and the teacher, and the teacher is signaling to them the very first day that he or she has faith in them. As an added bonus, this arrangement also allows a teacher to quickly create a circle for group discussions and works especially well for upper-level students.

For advanced classes, or classes where a great deal of class discussion takes place, a circle is the best arrangement. If you have a number of different classes, and only one or two classes where a circle seems appropriate, forming a circle for just those classes takes only a minute. Before long, your students will look forward to hearing you say the words, "Circle up for a class discussion." When using the circle method in your classroom, make sure that students understand the rules for a class discussion. These three rules seem to work the best:

1. Only one person is allowed to talk at a time, and no one is allowed to interrupt the person talking.
2. Everyone in the circle must make one contribution to the discussion before a student is allowed to talk again unless a specific question is directed to a specific student.
3. Everyone's opinion has value, and no one is allowed to make another student feel inferior in any way.

Try to be creative when you arrange the desks in your room. Think of all of your students, not just the one who wants to sit in the front or hide out in the back. Think about changing your arrangement again at the semester. Students get bored going from classroom to classroom and sitting in rows, and something simple like changing your desk arrangement can make the atmosphere of your classroom much more conducive to different learning styles.

BARE WALLS AND NO MONEY

Unless you were fortunate enough to take the place of a teacher who retired and left everything behind, the chances are good that you will find yourself looking at bare walls, wondering what to do to liven up the room. You will leaf through catalogs and eye beautiful posters wishing you could spend the money required to make your room interesting. Few schools will allocate substantial money for posters, but there are a few ways to make your room attractive without spending a great deal of money.

You must first accept the fact that sometimes your students will not be listening to you. Sometimes, their minds will wander or they will have free time and they will begin to look around the room. This is where you can guide them to ideas and quotations they may not actually comprehend until the middle of the year.

As a first-year teacher, money will be foremost in your mind. Most first-year teachers do not have extra money to spend on posters, nor do they feel confident enough to ask the principal or supervisor for the money. Try creating your own posters. The results may surprise you.

First of all, borrow a copy of *Bartlett's Quotations* from the library or log on to one of the many quotation sites on the Internet and spend some time looking for great quotations by authors whose words you want your students to recognize. Then, grab a stack of magazines and go to work. Cut out pictures of athletes, celebrities, and politicians that your students will recognize and try to match up the pictures with the perfect quotations. A picture of Shaquille O'Neal and Kobe Bryant can have the quotation "It was the best of times; it was the worst of times" written underneath. Today's technology will allow you to create these posters even more quickly. Be constantly on the lookout for new pictures and interesting quotations, and keep adding to your collection. Soon you will have enough posters to change them every so often and keep your students' interest. Have your posters laminated so that they will last for many years.

Teachers who have created their own posters often find that they receive rewards far beyond what they anticipated. A teacher who had made several of these posters explained how a student, who seemed to spend an inordinate amount of time staring at a poster she had made, finally began to understand the quotation's importance.

> I had created a poster that I thought was interesting. It involved a picture of a businessman in a trench coat walking down the street carrying a briefcase and looking at his watch. Next to his picture, I had written the following quotation: "No man is an Island, entire of itself; every man is a piece of the Continent, a part of the main; if a clod be washed away by the sea, Europe is the less, as well as if a promontory were, as well as if a manor of thy friends or of thine own were; any man's death diminishes me, because I am involved in Mankind; And therefore never send to know for whom the bell tolls; It tolls for thee."
>
> —John Dunne [1572–1631], Meditation XVII

This teacher explained what happened one day in her class.

> I remember clearly a student, sitting next to my desk, who looked at me a few seconds before the bell rang and said, "I finally get it! Wow! That's neat!" The bell rang, and he jumped up from his seat and left the room before I could even ask him what he was talking about. The next day I assigned free journal writing at the beginning of the hour. (I admit I was hoping this student would tell me what he finally got.) Later as I read his journal, I discovered two pages written on, as he called him, the No-Man-Is-An-Island Dude. This young

man had decided that many people go through life, simply living for their jobs and not realizing how they are affecting the people around them. It was one of the best pieces of writing he ever did, and he told me many years later that he had kept it.

This teacher had succeeded in opening her student's mind not only to a great quotation by a great author, but also to the excitement of taking that quotation and applying it in a way that made it personal to him. Moments like these are the ones that you will always treasure, the ones that will make teaching more than just a job. Another teacher shared a similar story with me:

"I had designed a poster of Laurence Olivier that showed him in major roles from the time he was a very young man to pictures from the movie *King Lear*, just pictures of him and the following lines:"

> All the world 's a stage,
> And all the men and women merely players.
> They have their exits and their entrances;
> And one man in his time plays many parts,
> His acts being seven ages. At first the infant,
> Mewling and puking in the nurse's arms.
> And then the whining school-boy, with his satchel
> And shining morning face, creeping like snail
> Unwillingly to school. And then the lover,
> Sighing like furnace, with a woful ballad
> Made to his mistress' eyebrow. Then a soldier,
> Full of strange oaths and bearded like the pard;
> Jealous in honour, sudden and quick in quarrel,
> Seeking the bubble reputation
> Even in the cannon's mouth. And then the justice,
> In fair round belly with good capon lined,
> With eyes severe and beard of formal cut,
> Full of wise saws and modern instances;
> And so he plays his part. The sixth age shifts
> Into the lean and slipper'd pantaloon,
> With spectacles on nose and pouch on side;
> His youthful hose, well saved, a world too wide

For his shrunk shank; and his big manly voice,
Turning again toward childish treble, pipes
And whistles in his sound. Last scene of all,
That ends this strange eventful history,
Is second childishness and mere oblivion,
Sans teeth, sans eyes, sans taste, sans everything.

—*As You Like It* Act ii. Sc. 7. W. Shakespeare

This teacher explained that few of her students ever took the time to read the entire poster, but some of them would read a few lines every day.

One day close to Winter Break, a young man looked at her and said, "Does the word *sans* mean *without?*" She assured him that it did, and after a few more moments, his face lit up and he said to her, "Wow! Do you know how good this Shakespeare guy is? That is an awesome poem! He's saying that a man goes in a circle and ends up as helpless as he was when he was a baby!"

The kind of satisfaction that you will receive as a teacher is nothing compared to the satisfaction that your students will have when they discover a wondrous quotation by a great writer. Not all of the learning in a classroom takes place in the traditional way. The lessons that you teach your students about life will be the lessons that will have the greatest impact on them long after they leave the safety of your classroom.

These posters can also be used to initiate class discussion. If you have a few minutes at the end of class time, choose a poster on the wall, read it to the class, and call on one of your students to start a discussion on what the quotation means and if it is still relevant today. Then step back and listen to what your students have to say. Try not to guide the discussion, even though you may be tempted to do so. Some of the best classroom discussions will occur after you have read one of these quotations out loud to the class and then given them the opportunity to discuss it as a group. The "No man is an Island" quotation works extremely well for this, as does "A little learning is a dangerous thing," (Pope) and "If a man does not keep pace with his companions, perhaps it is because he hears a different drummer. Let him step to the music which he hears, however measured or far away" (Thoreau). If this type of discussion does not work perfectly the first time, do not give up. Your

This brings up another important point—supplies. What should you do when a student shows up for class without the supplies he or she needs? First of all, no student ever did this on purpose in order to make the teacher mad; therefore, chastising a student for forgetting to bring an item to class is not a good idea. Instead, keep a supply of pens, pencils, highlighters, and paper nearby. Buy them in bulk; you will use them all. If a student needs one of these, handle it one of two ways, leaving the choice up to the student. The student can purchase these supplies (perhaps you could charge a dime for a pencil, a quarter for a pen or highlighter, and a dime for ten sheets of paper) or else the student can leave something with you for collateral until you get your pen or pencil back. You will get some interesting things for security, from packages of gum to shoes. The item used for collateral must be at least worth the cost of the item. If the student cannot do either of these, then he is at the mercy of his classmates for a loan. Sending a student back to his locker for the item is never a good idea, and if you simply hand a student a pen or pencil, nine out of ten times you will never see the item again. This is not always done on purpose; most students simply walk out of the room and forget to give it back. It is rather difficult, however, for him to walk out of your room without a shoe.

LEAVE IT AT THE DOOR

Students will often forget to bring items to your class, and many teachers make this an issue. Put yourself in your student's place, however, and don't make this a hill you want to die on. For the average English class, a student may have a grammar book and workbook, a literature book, a vocabulary book, and a novel. Telling them the day before what book they need to bring works for many students, but you can count on one thing—some students will forget. Time will be lost while students are sent to their lockers to get what they need for your class. Those bookshelves in your room can save you and your students time and aggravation. If you do not have bookshelves, use cubes that will stack so that you do not need much room to make this work. Label each cube or shelf according to which class period's materials are stored there. Keep all workbooks in this area. When they are needed, they can be quickly passed out to the students. Students can then take the workbooks home for the assignment and bring them back the following day, or they can do the assignment in class. The workbooks will always be there and they will stay in much better condition than they will in your students' lockers. Yes, you are trying to teach your students to be responsible, but other areas exist where you can make this a goal. This is not one of them.

CLUTTER, CLUTTER, EVERYWHERE, AND ALL THEIR THOUGHTS DID SHRINK

You will enter some classrooms belonging to other teachers that will look so cluttered and unorganized that you will wonder how this teacher ever finds anything. Some teachers apparently feel that the more things they have on their bulletin boards, chalk/white boards, walls, and desks, or hanging from their ceilings, the more impressed people will be by all the work that goes on in their classrooms, or perhaps this teacher simply hasn't made organization a priority. Many teachers, however, who appear unorganized can actually find anything in a matter of moments. Most teachers, though, have simply not made organization a priority, and finding things becomes something of a quest.

Promise yourself right now that you will *not* be one of these teachers. Even if you are not especially organized at home, your classroom can still be organized, neat, and orderly. An unorganized room will not only make your job much more difficult, but many students will also actually have a harder time concentrating because of the disarray. A few simple methods will insure that you can find things easily and quickly.

First of all, go to a discount store and invest in inexpensive plastic bins or trays to hold papers. If possible, have two bins for each class; if you are short on space, use one stackable tray with two folders in each tray for each class. One bin or folder is used to hold the day's homework, and the other one is used to hand back any work that you have graded for that class. Label each bin or folder clearly with a stick-on address label so that you can change the labels as your classes change from year to year. Rather than spending valuable class time collecting homework, instruct your students on the first day of class that it is their responsibility to put their assignments in the bin or folder at the beginning of the class period. You will only have to remind students of this for the first few weeks of school; after that, they will automatically turn their work in as soon as class begins.

When you are ready to grade homework, simply take the folder that you need and grade the papers. Then, transfer them to the "graded" folder. When you begin class, you can see at a glance whether or not you have work to pass back. Keep another bin for makeup work. In this bin place a folder for each class. When you hand out a worksheet or assignment, put the extra copies in the folder marked for that class. Another good idea is to quickly jot the absent student's name on the handout as well as the date. When a student returns, he knows to check the folder or bin for any handouts. By recording the date on the paper, you will know how many days pass before you receive the completed assignment. Most schools allow a student one day to make up work for each day that he or she misses. The few seconds that you take to do this will easily decrease the amount of time you need to spend with students who have been absent. Be as consistent as possible in this area and follow your school's policy for makeup work to the letter. Makeup work should be the responsibility of the student, not the teacher, and by explaining this to your students at the beginning of the year, you will be accomplishing two important things: they will become more responsible, and you will become more organized.

Once again, something that may seem somewhat insignificant in the grand design of your classroom, like makeup work and how you handle it, is actually quite important to the tone you are setting for your students. You are teaching them more than just your subject area; you are preparing them for a real world where failure to meet deadlines can have serious repercussions.

Before long that dreary, empty room the principal led you to on that first day will become *your room*. Every morning when you enter, you will look around with pride at the educational atmosphere you have created, an atmosphere that is creative without being overwhelming and organized without being stifling, an atmosphere that alerts your students to the idea that learning takes place here.

WEBSITES FOR QUOTATIONS

www.quotationspage.com
www.bartleby.com
www.quoteland.com
www.creativequotations.com

STAND BY YOUR PLAN

Building a Foundation for Learning

As a new teacher, you've probably been given plenty of advice already. Some of it seems silly: "Don't smile at your students until November," or "Start out tough; you can always let up later." Methods classes and fellow teachers, however, probably have not given you concrete advice about how to run a classroom where learning is a priority.

For the first few years, experiment with a variety of methods until you find one that challenges both you and your students to excel. Being a good teacher is hard work every single day; don't let anyone tell you differently. The following chapter will provide you with some guidelines on how to create an environment where your students understand that their education is important to you and that you will not be swayed from accomplishing your goals.

START THE DAY OFF RIGHT

Start class the same way every day. This may seem to contradict everything that you've heard, but your classroom needs to be structured, at least in some areas, and the time when class begins is one of these. By starting class the same way each day, your students know that when the bell rings, learning begins.

On Mondays, hand out a worksheet that students will work on all five days by doing a few problems at the beginning of class time each day. For an English class, working on two sentences a day that have writing and grammatical errors works well. For a math class, two or three problems on a worksheet or on the board should provide this initial focus; for biology, two important terms to look up in the back of the book would work; for a history class, looking up two important people or dates would be perfect. The most important part is that *every single day* students know that this is how class starts. If none of these seems to be something you feel is important, then have a brainteaser ready at the beginning of every class. Books and websites are available that have enough brainteasers to last an entire year. However you choose to begin your class, try beginning it the same way as soon as the bell rings or class officially begins.

For the first few weeks of school, as soon as the bell rings, remind your students to get out this worksheet or have the brainteaser ready to pick up as they walk into the room. While students are working on this, you will have time to take attendance and prepare for the hour. This should not take longer than two or three minutes at the beginning of your class time. Students can do these exercises independently or with a partner; for instance, on Tuesdays and Thursday they can work with a partner, on Mondays, Wednesdays, and Fridays, they work the problems out independently. After a few minutes, go over the answers with your students and then make the transition to your lesson plans for the day. At the end of the week, collect the papers and give students a completion grade for the work they have done all week. Students will always work harder when they know they will be held accountable for the work they do in your class.

During a time when teachers are being told to vary their instruction time and to try to find creative ways to get their students' attention, this type of plan seems doomed to failure, but it actually works. By the third week of class, most students will automatically get this paper out and begin working. They know what is expected of them. This will only work, however, if it is done *every day* at the beginning of the hour.

Teachers who have tried this are amazed at how well it works. The tone has been set that class begins when the bell rings, and students are prepared to learn. One teacher couldn't wait to tell me how well this had worked for her.

I didn't realize the full benefits of this until later in the year. I had been called to the office in between classes, and as I headed to my classroom, the bell rang. I was about ten yards from my room when I heard one of my students, a young man named Mitchell, say to the class (in a perfect imitation of me), "OK class, get your DOL (Daily Oral Language) out and do the sentences for today."

Curious, I decided to stand in the hall where they couldn't see me in order to see what would happen next. After a minute or so, Mitchell headed to the lectern where I keep the book that has the answers in it. I thought Mitchell was probably going to give the class all the answers so that they wouldn't have to think for themselves. Imagine my surprise when, instead, he spoke, again in a perfect imitation of my voice, and said, "Now, who wants to begin correcting the first sentence—Elizabeth? Thank you for volunteering."

I stood there listening to my class go through those two sentences as though I were in the room. As they were finishing up, I walked into the room and Mitchell, smiling, said to me, "It's okay, Mrs. B., I got ya covered. DOL's done."

My students could tell by the look on my face that their actions had surprised and pleased me.

This teacher was absolutely right. Deep down, most of your students want you to be happy with them. They do not want to let you down, and they want to meet your expectations. The attitude your students will take about the importance of their education will mirror the attitude that you take.

Students truly need and want to know what is expected of them. If they know your expectations, they are willing to try to live up to them. This method of starting class each day can work with any area of study. As a new teacher, you can expect an administrator or mentor teacher to observe you at least once a semester. How impressive for this person to see that when the bell rings, your students are ready to learn! Even more importantly, how impressive for your students to see that when the bell rings, you are ready for them to learn—every day.

FOR WHOM THE BELL TOLLS

If your school has a bell system that signals to your students that it's time to move on, you may find yourself tempted to let the bell dismiss your class.

Don't. Let your students know that the bell is a signal to *you* that they need to go. Explain to your students that they are to wait for *you* to verbally dismiss them. Why? This probably seems to you like a trivial matter, some sort of power struggle between teacher and class. It is not. Having students wait to be dismissed by you is a sign of respect. Often you will find that you are in the middle of assigning work for the next day when the bell rings. If students are not waiting for your dismissal, they will immediately run for the door, missing what you say. Teach them on the first day that they will have to wait for you to dismiss them, and be ready to back it up by standing at the door until they understand that you are serious. Again, you must be *consistent* about this.

Few teachers do this, and it's easy to understand why. Many feel that this is just another teacher-ego thing and completely unnecessary. Teaching your students to respect the adult in charge of the classroom, however, is important.

Teachers who decide to use this approach find that the benefits are immediate and obvious. A teacher from a small school in Indiana shares this story.

> A few years ago, when one of my classes was reading *Brave New World*, I contacted one of my former college professors and asked him to come and meet with my class. I thought the experience would be good for my students; they could see how a "real college professor" taught a class. When the day arrived for him to teach my class, I was more than a bit concerned. How would they act? Would they embarrass me in front of someone I respected? Would they pay attention? Would they ask good questions?
>
> I needn't have worried. My students were impressive. They asked probing questions and seemed intent on impressing him with their knowledge and maturity. Then the bell rang; class was over, and still he continued talking to them. I saw a few worried glances at the clock, but no one moved. More than a minute later, I saw an opening and explained to him that the students needed to get moving or they would be late for their next class. As a college professor, of course, this had never even occurred to him. He was used to students sitting there until he was done. As the class filed out of the room, he turned to me and said, "How long would they have sat there without telling me they had to go?"
>
> "Forever," I told him, prouder of them than I could even admit to myself.

This professor had driven an hour and a half—one way—to meet with my students in his free time. What message would they have sent if they had made a wild dash to the door when the bell rang?

When students behave appropriately, as these students did, it is important to commend them for their behavior and explain to them why this was so important to you.

This may seem hard for a new teacher to believe, but your students will be reassured by knowing that you are in charge, no matter what age they may be.

By setting the tone early in the year that she, and not the bell, was in charge of when her students could leave, this teacher had taught her students a valuable lesson about respect. A reminder, though: never make your students stay in their seats after the bell rings for some infraction that may have occurred during class time. Not dismissing them from class is not to be used as a punishment held over their heads. Use it only for the reason listed above—to let them know that you are finished meeting with them for the day.

IN BETWEEN HELLO AND GOOD-BYE

So far we have covered the way to begin and end your class. What about the minutes in between? What about teaching? What about grading? Homework? Discipline?

Well, that's a lot of ground to cover. First of all, two words do not belong in any teacher's vocabulary—*free day*. As a new teacher, your students will often come to you and say, "Can we have a free day today?" or "All the other teachers have given us a free day today; why can't you?" The temptation will be great to do just this. Some days you will feel overburdened with paperwork, lesson plans, and general catch-up. Resist this temptation if at all possible. Your students should quickly learn that you have something planned for them to learn every day. The time that they spend with you is too important to throw away, no matter how much you have to do or what everyone else seems to be doing.

Make a promise to yourself right now that you will demonstrate to your students how important their education is to you by always having something planned for them to learn. If you have to be absent from your class, make sure that you have emergency lesson plans on file that are productive for your students and can be handled easily by your substitute. Put some time and thought into these plans and make sure to update them as you change what you are teaching in your classes.

MAKING THE GRADE

Grading is another important part of your teaching, and one that you should take seriously. What assignments should you grade? How many grades should you take? What should a grade indicate? These are all excellent questions, and you should determine the answers before your first day of class.

If possible, avoid taking grades on work done outside your classroom, with the exception of papers that are written or projects that are completed. Instead, give a completion grade for homework, usually ten to twenty points, depending on the length of the assignment. Two good reasons exist for doing this. The first reason is the obvious one: how can you tell if a student has done the work on his own? The second reason is a better one: if you are teaching something new and want your students to do work outside of class to reinforce what you are teaching, then you can be sure that at least one student will tell you the next day that he didn't understand what the class was doing so he didn't do his homework. By giving only a completion grade, the student is encouraged to at least try to do the work, knowing that mistakes will not count against him. Again, homework should never be used as punishment; only assign homework as reinforcement for what you have covered during class time, and certainly, do not assign work every night.

WHAT DOES AN A MEAN TO YOU?

One of the hardest parts of being a teacher is assigning grades to the students in your class. In today's society, every student is supposed to be an honor student and assigning an F appears tantamount to scarring a child for life. An A on an assignment or for a class grade, however, should mean what it was originally intended to mean, that the student has accomplished excellence in his or her work. Likewise, a C is supposed to be the grade assigned to the student who has done average work. When did most of the educational system decide that an A meant that the student is well mannered, hardworking, and somewhat competent?

When a student gets an A in your class for an assignment, for the term, or for the semester, he or she should feel a sense of accomplishment. If you hand out As to a majority of your class, then either you are not teaching them enough, or you have bought into the "feel-good" theory of education. If everyone in your class gets an A, what sort of accomplishment does the A represent?

Students should expect to work hard for their As and for their Bs. These grades should be an accomplishment for the student, one of which he or she is proud. Be prepared, however, for complaints from the students who are used to getting As. They may find themselves initially confused by the idea that to their new teacher, an A is a sign of excellence. How tragic. As our government, our teacher associations, and our schools try to figure out how to solve the educational problems of today, perhaps a simple concept should be readopted. Challenge your students to work harder and show them the rewards when they do. The amazing part of this is how little time it takes students to realize that, to you, an A symbolizes that they have mastered what you have taught. The level of work that your students will do for you will increase in quality as soon as they realize that you are not "an easy mark." You are giving them back the sense of pride that comes from knowing that their grades truly reflect their knowledge and effort.

An F should actually be as hard to get in a class as an A. At the end of the grading term, you should have taken enough grades on in-class work that any student that wants to pass your class certainly can. Some of them, unfortunately, either don't seem to understand this or have been conditioned to believe that they will be passed on. Every term you will probably be faced with students who have earned an F in your class. Instead of passing them on, try to work with them and encourage them in whatever way you can. Make sure that they understand just where they are as far as achieving in your class and what they can do to improve. In the end, however, the decision to pass or fail must be theirs. Just as you have hopefully made the commitment that an A will mean something in your class, you must be equally committed to teaching the more difficult lesson—that you will not pass a student who does not deserve to pass. This will be the toughest decision you will ever make as a teacher.

AN EXPLANATION MAY BE IN ORDER

If you decide that an A or an F in your class should mean something, eventually you will be faced with an upset parent. This parent will question how his or her child, who has up until now always gotten As in your subject area, could possibly be getting a B or (perish the thought) a C. Equally difficult is explaining to a parent why a child is failing your class.

Dealing with parents is always tricky. Parents rarely realize that the teacher is as nervous talking to them as they are talking to the teacher. Remember that every parent that comes to see you in a conference brings with him or her every educational experience that he or she has ever had. Some of these will be positive ones; many, however, will be negative. You may be dealing with the class bully or the class valedictorian from twenty years ago. Most parents were, once upon a time, students themselves, and their memories of school may be present in their subconscious when they meet with you. First of all, greet the parent warmly and say something positive. Then, ask him or her what *his or her* goals are for the child. Listen carefully to the responses that you get so that you can more accurately gauge in which direction the conference needs to go. You need the parents of your students on your side. Accomplishing this will make your job easier and your student's educational experience better. If the parent simply wants to know why Amber is not getting an A, then explain this clearly by showing her Amber's grades on different assignments. If possible, show him or her examples of Amber's work compared to a student's work who received an A (obviously, the A paper must have the name removed from it). Make sure that the parent leaves with the understanding that you are trying to challenge this child into doing superior work and that you are willing to do everything that you can to allow Amber to succeed. For the parent whose child is failing, you should do the same things, but in addition, you should discuss alternatives to your class if it seems applicable. Try to figure out between the two of you possible reasons for the child's failure. Offer to talk to the counselor with the parent about the child's attitude toward school or his inability to succeed. Offer to keep in contact with the

parents of this child once a week or so and let them know how the child is doing well before the next grading period ends. Most importantly, assure the
parents that although their child may not be passing at the moment, you are
not going to give up, that you will work with them to help the child succeed.

Finally, don't get caught up in your school's valedictorian race or in making sure Brandon's grades get him into Purdue or an exclusive liberal arts
school. Instead, get caught up in preparing Brandon to succeed when he gets
to college and for life after that. Don't let yourself be pressured by parents
who think their children are geniuses or by administrators with hidden agen-
das. Keep your eyes on your real goal: preparing your students to succeed in
a world that doesn't know their parents, their grandparents, or even their
older brother, a world where "pretty good" simply isn't good enough.

MY WAY OR THE HIGHWAY?

Discipline is one of the hardest parts of education for a beginning teacher.
Methods vary from check marks on the board to a detention. If a new teacher
follows these six strategies, however, he or she will find that discipline problems will be few and far between.

1. Do not try to be your students' friend.

    Everyone, especially a first-year teacher, wants to be liked. You
    must get over this. Your students already have friends, and even if they
    don't, what they need from you is an education, not a buddy. Many
    teachers try to win over their classes by allowing a casual, relaxed at-
    mosphere to exist between them and their students. By doing this you
    will certainly become known as one of the "coolest teachers in the
    school," but your students, though they make like you, will certainly
    not respect you. Once again, remember your goal is to educate your
    students. You cannot do this if they feel that you are equals. You are
    not equals, or at least you certainly shouldn't be.

    Choosing not to be your students' friend is not the same thing as
    being friendly to your students. A fine line exists between being com-
    passionate, caring, and approachable to your students and being
    friends with your students. Many of your students do not have an

adult in their lives that they feel cares about them or wants to listen to them. You may be the only adult that they trust. This is fine; just be careful to keep the relationship within its proper boundaries.

2. Let your students know that their education is important to you and you will allow nothing to stand in your way.

Simple things, like the note on your door mentioned in chapter 2, have already signaled this to them. Now you can prove it in other ways. Be ready and eager to start class each day. Use energy in your teaching, even if you are teaching the same thing for the third time that day. Never complain about the school, other teachers, your love life, or your bills. Always stay focused on the most important thing—teaching your class. One of the hardest parts about being a teacher is also the most important. You must be committed to educating your students at the very highest level they can achieve. Once they understand how seriously you take their education, they will appreciate what you are doing for them.

3. Use every minute of your class time productively.

A large percentage of classroom discipline problems occur during "downtime." If your lesson plans only take fifteen minutes to cover, you will have discipline problems. If you hand your students a stack of worksheets every day for them to do while you work on other things, you will have discipline problems. Although your students may act like it isn't so, they hate having their time wasted. When students aren't engaged in *active* learning, the class drags on forever. Always have the full class period covered, even if you spend the last ten minutes reviewing those vocabulary words on the posters on the wall or asking them to do a last-minute journal entry. Let them know that you feel you cannot waste a minute of your time with them. They will respect you for it.

4. Handle student problems immediately and do not let them interfere with your teaching.

Problem students enjoy disrupting class. Don't let them. In most schools teachers are allowed to assign a detention whenever they feel one is warranted. As a student's detentions mount, the punishment becomes more severe and is handled by the administrator. Find out exactly what the procedure is in your school. Keep a list of detention referrals in a handy place. If a student behaves inappropriately, do not stop class and address the problem, simply walk to your desk (as you continue teaching), retrieve a discipline referral, write it out, hand it to the student, and continue teaching. Explain to your students on the first day of class that this will be your procedure and that you will not interrupt your teaching to confront their bad behavior. If they wish to talk about the situation, tell them you will gladly do so at the end of the class period. If a student persists in disrupting the class, then the student must be immediately removed from the class according to the procedures dictated to you by your supervisor. You will usually not have to do this more than once for any class. By using this method, you are in control of your classroom problems immediately, instead of letting your classroom problems control your classroom. The hardest thing to do as a new teacher is to do this the very first time. Warnings are a bad idea; your students were warned the first day of class. If you cannot be consistent, then this method will not work for you.

5. Never humiliate or embarrass a student.

This cannot be stressed strongly enough. Be careful how you address a student when you are attempting to change his or her behavior. Concentrate solely on the behavior and not on the individual. You do not want to make any confrontation personal. Humiliating or embarrassing a student, especially in your classroom, will be counterproductive to everything you are trying to accomplish.

6. One simple statement for your classroom will take care of everything.

Some teachers have a list of rules in their classrooms that student are expected to follow. Most of these are the same rules students have been expected to follow since they began attending school. Posting a list of rules for your classroom can also be counterproductive. Obviously, you cannot address every situation that comes up, and posting rules is a rather negative way to create a positive learning environment. Instead, place a simple statement somewhere in your room that handles every situation. This can become a mission statement for your classroom, a much more positive reminder than a list of regulations. For example, "In this room *nothing* will stop us from learning."

One last word or two of encouragement for new teachers: if you follow the strategies listed here, your first year may still be a tough one as students try to test you to see if you are really serious. However, students quickly spread the word about which teachers can and cannot control their classrooms and which teachers are truly interested in providing them with a quality education. Students will come to your classroom in the future already knowing what to expect. Build a strong foundation for learning in your classroom with consistency and consideration.

WEBSITES FOR DAILY BRAINTEASERS

www.brainbashers.com
www.billsgames.com/brain-teasers/
www.braingle.com
www.mentalmaniacs.com

4

SCHOOL'S OUT

Being Involved in After-School Activities

Unlike most jobs, being a teacher is rarely a nine-to-five career. Chances are good that sometime during your interview, one of the administrators will ask you to coach a team, sponsor a club, or be on a committee. Some of these opportunities even come with a cash incentive. What should you do when asked to participate in after-school activities?

Obviously, you should consider your options carefully; however, before agreeing to become involved with anything outside the classroom, ask yourself these three important questions: Do I have the knowledge? Do I have the time and energy? Do I want to do this for the next fifteen or twenty years?

I TEACH; THEREFORE, I COACH

Some teachers go into teaching with the idea that they also want to coach. They have planned for this and are looking forward to the coaching aspect of the job. Other new teachers, however, are totally unprepared for any type of coaching but may feel that turning down the offer to coach middle school girls' volleyball may harm their chance for the job. A new teacher who had just finished her student teaching in a high school near the town where she lived shared this story: "I felt that I had done a great job student teaching, and when a job opened up in the middle school, I was pretty confident that I would get it. The principal knew my family and had watched my brother and me play sports at a nearby county school. The interview went extremely well, and we had an interesting conversation as we discussed people that we both knew and my enthusiasm for beginning a teaching career. I was sure that he would offer me the job."

She was surprised at the comment the principal made at the conclusion of the interview: "He said that he was sure that I would want to coach like my dad and brother and informed me that there was an opening in middle school girls' basketball and that he would put me down for that, too. I had absolutely no desire to coach; I was only interested in being a teacher. When I told him this, his attitude towards me immediately changed. He quickly concluded our interview, and I never heard from him again."

If you are asked to coach a team during your interview and you are not sure you want to do this, then do not feel you have to commit right away. A good answer to the request is to say, "I had never really considered coaching (girls' volleyball). Can I have a few days to think about it?" Then, take the time to do just that. Ask yourself if you feel that you can be a competent coach. Did you play the sport in high school or college? Do you have someone in mind that would be willing to help you? How do you feel about spending two hours a day for three months in the school gym? Will arriving home from an away game at 11:30 at night affect your ability to teach the next day? Can you ride on a bus for two hours with twenty-five screaming adolescents? Most of all, ask yourself this important question: Will coaching make me a better teacher? For some, the answer will be yes; for many, the answer will be no.

If you plan to be a teacher and a coach, then please be a teacher in the classroom and a coach on the playing field. Many coaches are fine teachers, but there are also many teacher-coaches who cannot seem to keep these two jobs separate. Your preparation time at school should be spent preparing for your classes and not for your games. When students see that you spend class time preparing for sports activities, then you are sending them the message that coaching comes first for you. Why, then, should your class and the work they do for you be important to them? Also, although you know your players much better than you know your students, in the classroom be conscious of the fact that all students should be treated equally and that students are watching to see if you are consistent. You cannot be an effective teacher if your students see that you give preferential treatment to your athletes. Be aware of your responsibilities to all of your students. You can be an excellent teacher *and* an excellent coach.

AN OPENING BID OF TWO CLUBS

This is the section of the book that the veteran teachers at your new school do not want you to read. As a matter of fact, if word gets out, this veteran teacher ploy may cease to exist. This ploy is called "Let's Sucker the New Teacher into Taking over This Club."

Every year at the first staff meeting, usually before school actually starts, the principal enters the meeting with *The List*. The veteran teachers will visibly cringe and avoid making eye contact with the principal, while the new teachers look at him with anticipation and eagerness in their eyes. *The List* contains the clubs, organizations, and class sponsorship openings. Be very careful about signing *The List*. Teacher sponsorship is an important part of your job, and you should certainly be willing to help out where you can, but do not rush into anything at this time. Signing your name next to a club may very well mean that you will be the sponsor of that club for the next twenty years. The veteran teachers know this, the second-year teachers know this, and they also know that as a new teacher you will be willing and eager to fit in with your new school. They count on it, and they are never wrong. The openings that seem to occur every year at most schools are the junior class sponsorship (because of the prom), the student council sponsorship (because of the abundance of activities), and the yearbook or school paper (because of the sheer amount of work involved).

This is the type of discussion you will probably hear:

"I really enjoyed sponsoring the yearbook last year (last year's new teacher will say), but because of the new baby, I feel that I just don't have the time this year. I'll be more than glad to *help* whoever takes it, but I'm afraid I'll have to let someone else take it this year."

All eyes will then look at you.

You will be tempted to say, "I'll try it!"

The conversation may also sound like this:

"I learned a lot doing the prom last year, and this year's junior class is really excited about fundraising (don't believe *that* for a minute), but I've decided to coach the golf team this year, and so I won't be able to work on the prom because it is at the same time as golf season. I've got all my notes and contacts from last year, so this year should be a lot easier. I promise I'll help whoever takes it, but I just can't commit to it this year."

All eyes will be looking at you.

You will be tempted to say, "That sounds like fun!"

Think very carefully before you say a word. Do not make eye contact with the principal or last year's sponsor. Act like you are jotting down notes to yourself on a piece of paper. If you are asked point blank to take on a class, committee, or club that you are not positive you will enjoy, then take a deep breath, calmly meet the eyes of all present and say the following words: "It sounds like a great opportunity, but as a first-year teacher, I think I need to concentrate on just my teaching for the first year. Let me get a year under my belt and maybe I can try that next year."

How can a fellow teacher or principal argue with that logic? You have been saved . . . for the moment.

During the year, pay attention to each of these clubs and study the time that appears to be required for them. The next year you will be able to make an informed decision about what you do with your out-of-school time. The decision as to which clubs or activities you will supervise is an important one. Be sure to choose an activity that you will enjoy.

Remember, next year there will be probably be a *new* first-year teacher and the game will start anew. You will be a veteran.

TAKE ME OUT TO THE BALLGAME

As a teacher, you have already committed to more than an eight-hour workday. Many evenings will be spent preparing lessons, grading papers, and keeping up on the reading for your classes. As a first-year teacher, you will also be busy organizing your lesson plans and strengthening your knowledge in your subject area. Your students have schoolwork to do every night, too, but they also have another area that you should be aware of—extracurricular activities.

Make the effort to attend as many after-school events as you can. Your students need to see a different side of you, a side that supports them and enjoys watching them perform in an area that they actually enjoy. Many of your students have parents who work nights and are unable to come to their activities. Seeing you in the stands, standing up and cheering their names, makes them feel like you are interested in their lives, not just in their performance in your classroom. Band, chorus, drama, sports, and many other activities are an important part of many of your students' lives, and your effectiveness as a teacher, as well as their effectiveness as students, can be greatly enhanced by your attendance at their events.

Another reason for attending these events is so that you will have a greater understanding of what your students face outside of the classroom. The pressures and conflicts that they face in the sporting arena may sometimes find their way into your classroom, and understanding why a student may be acting a certain way will help you know best how to deal with that student.

In addition, you will begin to realize how much or how little time your students have available in the evenings for work that you assign to them. Many teachers have the attitude that their responsibility ends in the classroom and that the students must learn to manage their time if they want to be in activities. Not only is this unrealistic, it is also unfair. This type of teacher penalizes the very kids who are the most receptive to education. You do not have to always plan your classroom lessons around extracurricular activities, but you should certainly try to be aware of them. If you schedule a test for the day after an away game that is being played two hours from home, you are setting both you and your students up for disappointing results.

A teacher explains an incident that was an eye-opener for her in this area:

It was about 9:00 in the evening, and I had already eaten dinner, done a few loads of laundry, and was just settling in to do the reading that I had asked my class to do for the next day when I realized that I had left the book I needed at school. I drove to the school and was amazed to see quite a few cars in the parking lot. I went into the school to get my book and upon seeing one of the janitors, asked her whose cars were in the parking lot. When she told me that the cars were those of the girls on the basketball team who were playing a game in Terre Haute, I was shocked! Terre Haute was over an hour away! When would they get home? The janitor stated that she expected them to get home around 11:00 or 11:30. As I walked back to my car, I realized that the chances of the girls who were in my class that were also on the team getting their reading done by the next day were slight. After that, I always checked the boys' and girls' sports schedules before I assigned an hour of difficult reading or a lengthy test. As teachers, we should be understanding and encouraging of our students who want to be well-rounded. Obviously, I did not simply quit assigning work that needed to be done; instead I organized my difficult assignments around their schedules. Everyone benefits!

Another teacher relates how her attendance at her students' events translated over into the classroom. She was an avid tennis fan and had begun going to her students' tennis matches. Three of the starters for the boys' tennis team were in her dual-credit composition class, and they always looked forward to seeing her at their matches and hearing her comments the next day at school. After a strong beginning to the season, the team had a chance to win the conference title against their arch rivals from the next town. The boys had decided that this teacher was their "good luck" charm and, on the day of the match, checked with her to see if she would be there. "I was looking forward to seeing the match," she later recalled, " and was quite shocked to discover during class that day that none of the tennis players had done his reading for the day." She decided to skip their tennis match as a way of showing them that class work comes before athletics.

> I told them that I wouldn't be able to make it to the match that day because I was too disappointed in their lack of preparation for my class to cheer them on. They could tell how disappointed I was, both by their lack of preparation and to be missing their match. It was one of the hardest lessons I ever taught to a group of students. The boys realized, though, that I was right. They had to be athletes and scholars before I could be teacher and fan. For the rest of the year, even after tennis was over, those three young men came to class prepared every single day. At the end of the year, one of them gave me a tennis highlights video with parts of the big match on it. He told me. "We felt so bad that day. We knew how much you liked watching us play and we knew why you were doing what you did; we learned that letting someone down who cared enough to come out and watch us play was a terrible feeling."

As a teacher, you can teach your students some lessons that have nothing to do with the classroom and everything to do with life.

5

BY THE TIME I
GET TO PHOENIX

Teachers and Out-of-Class Time

Educational conferences, committee meetings, and generally anything that takes you or your students out of your classroom can be harmful to the educational environment you are trying to create. You need to be prepared to turn down many so-called opportunities that will come your way and take you out of the classroom. In addition you need to accept the fact that some students will try to convince you that (1) they need to be in your room at other times during the school day or (2) they do not need to be in your room during class time. Keeping yourself and your students where you both need to be is an integral part of the educational process.

YOU ARE CORDIALLY INVITED

Every year, you will receive at least fifteen to twenty invitations in your mailbox at school to attend various conferences. The number of these invitations seems to be increasing dramatically each year. As educational problems continue to receive national attention, an increasing number of conferences that claim they can solve the problems of education have sprung up with disturbing frequency. Most of them take place during school time, and all of them guarantee to make you a more effective teacher. A good teacher spends as much time as possible in the classroom teaching her students. One definite way to increase education in our schools is for the teachers to be present in their classrooms, teaching their students every day.

Just ten years ago, teachers rarely went to conferences or attended events during the school year. If a teacher was absent, she was either very sick or had a family emergency. Today, it is not unusual for half of the teachers in a building to be gone, most of them attending conferences or workshops. This means that half of the staff on those days consists of substitute teachers. For some students, it also means that they spend the entire day under the supervision of substitutes. Although most schools have excellent substitutes that fill in when they are needed, most of them will tell you that all they ever do is babysit while students do worksheets or watch a movie.

As a new teacher, you will receive many opportunities to attend conferences, and your principal may even encourage you to attend. Answer these three questions before you commit to leaving your classes:

1. Does this fit with a convenient time in your curriculum, or will you be losing an important day of class time? In other words, can you schedule a test for this day so that your students will not feel that they are wasting their time in your classroom?
2. Is the information that you will receive something that you cannot learn any other way?
3. Have you already missed too many days this term because of sickness and emergencies?

Think back to your high school days. Think back to what happened in your classes when a substitute teacher was there. Remember how exciting it was? Why? Because you knew you probably weren't going to do anything that day. Now remember how bored you were after the first fifteen minutes? Remember how long that class period seemed to take?

Try this experiment. If you have a younger brother or sister, or someone you can ask that is attending school, have him or her keep a journal for three weeks. In this journal ask the student to record two things: how many times in three weeks a substitute teacher took the place of the regular teacher and what the class did during that time.

You will be surprised at the number of hours many of our students spend watching movies, playing games, and doing worksheets meant to use up time.

Your students should be surprised and concerned when you do not show up for school. They should expect to see you there every day. Why? Because what you are doing in your classroom is important and you have already told them this and shown them this many times throughout the year. They will only believe this, however, if they see you there, teaching them the best way that you can, every day.

If you expect your students to buy into your belief that their education is important, then you must show them by your actions that this is true, no matter how tempting it may be to get away for a few days.

LET'S GO FLY A KITE

Field trips are another area where schools and many teachers seem to have lost their way. Every teacher thinks his or her field trip is an important one. If you are considering a field trip with your class or classes, first of all, reread the list above that discusses the reasons that *you* should leave the classroom, and then multiply the importance of these reasons by thirty or more. In other words, remember that you are taking students out of other teachers' classes, too.

Realize that your field trip is actually a terrible inconvenience to the other staff members and students in your school. Teachers have difficulty teaching a class when a high percentage of students are not there. The temptation to give a "free day" is great, and when you multiply that by six or seven class periods in a day, you can see what the students who are left behind are learning—very little. Unless the field trip your students are taking is something that they need to experience and can experience in no other way, you are better off finding alternatives.

If you have decided that a field trip is in order, give the teachers in your corporation plenty of notice. No matter how much notice your school may require, two weeks is the minimum amount of notice that you should give your fellow teachers. This may mean that you have to pass on a good opportunity once in a while, but remember that your fellow teachers usually have their lesson plans in mind a week or two in advance. Giving them only a day or two of advance warning is completely unprofessional and will signal to them, whether you mean to or not, that you feel that what they are doing "really isn't that important."

THE COURTESY OF A REPLY IS REQUESTED

As a new teacher, your students will try various methods to manipulate you. Two of these can cause serious conflicts between you and other teachers. Be aware of these two student strategies and have a plan in store for when (not if) they occur.

The first strategy is the "We're not doing anything anyway" strategy. At some point, one of your students will come to you and say something like this: "Since we're not doing anything in biology today, will you write me a pass so that I can come to your room and work on my project?"

Now, as a teacher you will be impressed that Jordan wants to work on her project. You will be impressed that she will give up free time so that she can do work for you.

You may then proceed to write a pass to her teacher that says something like this: "If you are not doing anything in your class today, Jordan has my permission to come to my room and work on her project."

Never write that pass. Think of the insult you are inadvertently giving to this teacher. Even if the teacher is, indeed, not planning to do anything, he or she cannot help resenting the fact that you know about it and are planning to remedy the situation by giving this student something to do. Nothing will negatively affect your relationships with the other teachers in your building more quickly than writing students passes to get out of their classes.

On the other hand, a teacher may do this to you someday. If Stacey brings you a pass from another teacher that asks you to let Stacey come and finish a project in her room, politely deny the request unless you feel it is definitely in Stacey's best interest to leave your room, for instance, if Stacey has been sick and has a test to make up, is working on a special exhibit, or has another valid reason why this work must be done during your class time. Once you become known as a teacher who will let her students leave the room, you will be inundated with requests from your students to do exactly that.

Along the same lines is allowing your students to be late to the next class because they are finishing a test. If a student needs less than five minutes more, then you can usually allow the student to stay. At the end of that time, write a pass, collect the test, and decide whether to allow the student more time the following day, during lunch, or after school to finish. If more than two or three students have not finished the test at the end of class time, then the test you have given is probably too long, and you should probably either eliminate the last few questions and collect the test or grade the students on the part that was completed.

It is not fair for you to take up another teacher's class time by allowing students to enter class late. Your fellow teachers may never know of your thoughtfulness, but they will definitely remember your rudeness.

THE IMPOSSIBLE DREAM

Much of what is written in this chapter is not the conventional method in many schools. Teachers are taught to be flexible and to work with each other to make our students' lives easier. How do you think this idea is working so far? Are teachers today teaching better than they were ten years ago because of all the conferences they attend? Is arranging our schedules to please our students making them better students?

A good teacher is one who puts her students' education first, each and every minute that they are in her room.

6

IF YOU COULD
READ MY MIND

Changes, Challenges, and Choices

Education classes and teaching seminars often concentrate on the importance of reaching a wide variety of students by using numerous teaching
techniques that are designed to reach the diverse learning styles of today's
students. At least eight different learning styles have been documented—
from kinesthetic to naturalist to spatial and so on. Few teachers ever truly understand how to implement each of these techniques; therefore, most simply
continue to fall back on what they think they do best. These complex strategies that are touted as the answer to all educational woes can actually be bro-
ken down into three much simpler areas: what students *hear*, what students
see, and what students *remember*.

A famous line from George Orwell's *1984* is "I understand how; I do not
understand why." Aldous Huxley's *Brave New World* centers on a society
where people are trained to do only certain things well; they understand that
they are all cogs in the wheel, but they have no clue as to the function of the
wheel. Students need to understand why, and more importantly, they need to
have the *desire* to understand why.

As a teacher, the most important function you serve is to teach your students how to think for themselves. Teaching students to be lifelong learners
is the greatest gift you can give them. Successful teaching starts with successful communication; a person who is extremely knowledgeable in his or

her field yet lacks the power to communicate that knowledge will have difficulty achieving success in the classroom.

Communication is the key to all knowledge, regardless of the subject area or the age level. How can a teacher learn to communicate better with students? What types of communication work best in the classroom? Knowing the answers to these two questions and applying them to the classroom will make all the difference in the quality of the students' education.

First of all, communicating well with students begins with what they *see* while they are in the classroom. Does this mean that the simple lecture method that many teachers use is doomed to failure? Absolutely not. In many cases, the lecture method is not only appropriate but also essential. The key to using the lecture method successfully, however, does not lie in how many pages of notes the students take, but what they remember from those notes when they leave the room.

LECTURE MODE

To begin with, no student has ever sat in a classroom and enjoyed listening to a teacher drone on and on while the student attempts to write down what he or she thinks the teacher feels is important. Change the traditional way of lecturing into one that works much better for students. For instance, if you are lecturing on the mistakes that Robert E. Lee made during the battle of Gettysburg, instead of giving students a list of these to write down, have the students get into groups of three and ask each group to come up with five or six mistakes. Then ask a member of the group to list on the board the mistakes they wrote down. In a typical classroom, you will have seven or eight groups. When each group has written its answers on the board, have the students look through all of the answers and find the ones that each group has in common. Simple things like placing check marks next to these will reinforce the common themes. Make a class list that shows the top responses for the question. This should be very close to the list you intended to give the class. Add the few that they may have missed, and your students have helped you in creating the list of mistakes rather than simply writing down what you have said. They will now remember much more clearly what Robert E. Lee's mistakes were. Why? They saw them on the board. They processed the results by grouping them, and finally, yet most importantly, they were involved in thinking up what the mistakes were in the first place. Instead of simply *hearing* the information, they have seen it and heard it, and now they will remember it.

Test this concept yourself. One day, give lecture notes as usual. The next day when class starts have the students answer a simple question that will show what they learned from your lecture. In the example above, you would ask them to write down all the mistakes they can think of that Robert E. Lee made in the battle of Gettysburg. Try the same thing after using the alternative to the lecture method. The difference in their recall will be apparent. The students using the group lecture method will have much better recall.

PUTTING IT ALL ON THE LINE

Sometimes, teachers simply have to give notes to their students. They have information that is critical to the subject and only the lecture method will do. Again, challenge yourself to change the method that you have seen time and time again in your own education. How? One simple way is to make an outline form for the students to fill in as you talk. This requires you to plan ahead, but the academic rewards for your students will be worth the extra time and effort you have spent. For instance, if you are teaching a literature class and the students need to know the qualities of Romantic literature as well as famous authors of the period and their most noted works, give your students an outline that guides them as they take notes on each of these categories. Do not give in to the temptation of filling all of this or even some of this in for them. Students rarely learn anything from a handout that already has everything on it they are supposed to know. They must interact with the material in order to process what you need them to know. Simply provide them the heading and the proper letters and numbers that correspond with the outline you want them to make. Many students actually enjoy doing this, and they definitely learn better by writing what you say in an organized way. Again, your students are seeing ideas come together as they fill in the outline form, and this promotes much better learning.

Two important points need to be remembered when you use the outline method. The first one is that you need to have a word bank on the board. Before class you should write down in the corner of the board any words that your students might have difficulty spelling, words that are unfamiliar to them. In the case of Romantic literature, the names Coleridge and Wordsworth would definitely need to be written down ahead of time. Try to limit the number of words to only those words that 75 percent of the students will have difficulty spelling. By having a word bank, students will not constantly interrupt class by asking how to spell certain words, and the spellings for these words become your students' responsibility.

Another important part of the outline lecture method is to *lead* students to the outline rather than telling them. Your students need to learn to listen carefully for the transition words and clues that you give them in creating their outline. Rather than telling them, for instance, to put the name Wordsworth under the Roman numeral one and Coleridge under Roman numeral two, say, "Two men began what was essentially the Romantic Movement in England. The first of these men was William Wordsworth, and the second one was Samuel Taylor Coleridge. Each of these men contributed three important concepts to the theory of Romanticism."

If you have formed your outline correctly, students should see something like this:

Important Writers of Romanticism and Their Contributions

    I.
      A.
      B
      C.
    II.
      A.
      B.
      C.

Learning to outline lectures is an extremely important tool for your students, especially for those who will attend college after graduation. Once again, you are teaching them to make connections, and you are allowing them to create something with you instead of simply listening to you and randomly writing down what you have to say.

THE HIGHLIGHT OF THE DAY

Highlighting is another important tool that your students need to utilize in order to be active learners. Some textbooks already have important points highlighted for the students, but studies show that this type of highlighting has no impact on what a student remembers from the text. When the student does the highlighting himself, however, reinforcement of the material does take place. Supplement your textbook with articles from magazines, journals, or Internet sources so that students can practice highlighting main points in their reading. Have students use highlighters when doing workbook assignments whenever possible. Students enjoy highlighting; it reminds them of the "good old days" when they were simply required to color and paste. When giving a test, have students highlight the directions for each section of the test. Many students never actually read the directions at the top of the page, and by having them highlight the directions, you will be helping them establish an important habit. The more highlighting your students do, the better they will become at comprehending and remembering what they have read.

LEFT BEHIND OR TOO FAR AHEAD

Another important key to successfully communicating with your students is to challenge them. You cannot simply serve up all of your ideas to your students and expect them to apply them. They must interact with you in the pursuit of knowledge—*passive* and *learners* are not words that should be used together in your classroom. In most classes a teacher will have a wide variety of students, many of them at different levels. How do you challenge the students who clearly need to be challenged without losing those students who are simply keeping their heads above water? Accomplishing this is one of the greatest and most important challenges a teacher faces. A math class is the perfect example of this. In math, students tend to divide up quickly: those who can understand each new idea quickly and those who have struggled since the day that letters began representing numbers.

This division usually brings about a few problems. The students who comprehend more quickly usually end up becoming bored while the teacher goes over the new concept once more. The students who didn't get it the first time are probably still having problems. Time is wasted, and nothing is being accomplished. A few solutions do exist, however, and they can be easily implemented into any classroom.

One good solution, and an obvious one, is to divide up the class into at least two, perhaps three groups: those who need a new challenge, those who need a bit more help, and those who are completely lost. One thing that you do not want to do is give the students at the top extra work. Many of them see this as punishment for having learned so quickly, and they resent it. These students should, instead, be spending time supplementing their education by learning how to use their brains in other ways. This is another place where your brainteasers can come in handy. Allow these students to work in groups of two or three and give them some tough brainteasers (see websites in chapter 3). Explain to them that they will be given a daily in-class grade based on their work in this area, while the other students are being graded on their work in the repeated area. This will give you time to work individually with the students who are lost.

The important strategy here is that you make time to work individually with students who are lost and that you give the students who have mastered your lesson something fun and educational to do. The students in the slower group are always excited when they are able to join the brainteaser group. Grouping your students will definitely be a challenge, but to do otherwise in this situation would mean letting someone down who is counting on you.

CHOOSING TO LEARN

Finally, a good teacher will often give his or her students choices. When students are allowed to choose a method of learning, much more learning will take place. For instance, if your objective is for students to understand similes and metaphors, then allowing students to choose how to present a simile or metaphor would greatly enhance both the student's understanding of figurative language and the class's understanding as well.

Some students are natural list makers. This type of student would want to create a poster that simply lists as many metaphors or similes as he or she can find or think of.

If the topic were love, then the student would want to write down things like this:

"Love is blind."

"Love is like an ocean."

"Love is like a perfect summer day."

A student drawn to music, however, would prefer to write a poem or song that expresses love, and a student who takes pleasure in drawing would enjoy creating a poster that shows a picture of the metaphor or simile.

Whenever possible, allow your students to show you how creative they can be by telling them what you want them to understand and then allowing them to create a form of understanding that works for them.

Implementing some or all of these teaching methods will take some time. Focus on those that you would be comfortable doing in your classroom. No teaching method works if the teacher is not comfortable presenting it. Challenge your students by letting them know that you expect them to come to your class prepared to meet you at a high level of learning. Change your method of presenting material so that you are reaching a wider audience. Give students choices whenever possible so that they can learn in a way that is more beneficial to them. You cannot read your students' minds, but you can use what you know about your students to open their minds to learning.

7

BURN, BABY, BURN

Avoiding Teacher Burnout

One of the reasons so many educators leave the teaching profession is because they become burned out. Teaching ceases to be the fulfilling career that they thought it would be, and the effort of teaching no longer holds any appeal. Most teachers who leave the profession do so after less than seven years. Why? What causes these teachers to turn their backs on what they previously thought would be the ideal climate for them? What can you, as a new teacher, do to prevent this from happening to you? What are the signs that signal you may be approaching teacher burnout?

The signs of teacher burnout are usually easy to recognize. A teacher approaching burnout may become depressed on Sunday night as he or she begins contemplating another week of school. Another sign is failure to prepare solid lesson plans that will benefit the students in the classroom. One of the most noticeable signs is a lack of enthusiasm toward students, the school, and even teaching. Finally, giving excuses is one of the most obvious signs. A teacher may tell him- or herself, "Nothing I do seems to make a difference," or "Why do I even try?" This is a definite red flag that a teacher needs to step back and reevaluate his or her attitude toward teaching.

One way to avoid teacher burnout is by studying those who seem to face this problem often as compared to those who seem never to be affected by burnout at all. First of all, the amount of years one has taught has no real bearing on teacher burnout; it can occur just as easily in a teacher's first year as it can in a teacher who has been teaching "burnout free" for twenty years. The environment one teaches in does not seem to be an indicator either. Teachers who teach in what many consider the perfect school system find themselves burned out as often as teachers who are in more challenging environments. Grade level, administrators, difficulty of schedule—none of these seem to be red flags signaling that a teacher is more likely to find herself wanting to change careers. The main source of teacher burnout can be attributed to one area—expectations.

What are your expectations as you begin your first year of teaching? Expectations are quite different from goals. Goals are something that your principal or department head asks you to write down in order for you to evaluate your progress throughout the school year. Expectations are the ideas that you bring with you into the classroom on your very first day of teaching. They are hoped-for realities that you have decided are important in order for you to feel successful as a teacher. When a new teacher's expectations are in line with the realities of teaching, avoiding teacher burnout is much easier.

HERE IN THE REAL WORLD

One of the first unrealistic expectations that a new teacher may have is that teachers are respected persons in the community and in the classroom. Twenty or thirty years ago this was, to a large extent, true. In today's world, however, teachers definitely do not enjoy this type of across-the-board treatment. Most young people who go into teaching today were themselves good students. They understood the value of education, and they understood the importance of a teacher; therefore, they believed that when they became teachers, they would also enjoy this measure of respect. When this does not happen, they blame it on the youth of today, wring their hands in frustration, and walk away convinced that nothing can be done to improve education as long as teachers are not given the respect they deserve.

Why is teaching as a profession given less respect than it was in years past? The question should actually be—what have teachers done to earn respect? Today's generation is mostly a product of parents and grandparents who were raised in an environment overshadowed by the Vietnam War, Watergate, church and corporate scandals, and rapid increases in single-parent homes. People no longer blithely trust the assurances of those in charge that everything is under control. They have seen for themselves the abuses of power, and they are leery of putting their faith and trust in those who have proven they are not trustworthy. In other words teachers today must prove themselves trustworthy; they must earn the trust of their students and their parents. By expecting this trust to be given before it is earned, many new teachers are setting themselves up for disappointment.

By realizing that you must earn the trust of those around you, you will not become frustrated when your students or their parents do not initially give you the respect you expect. How can you begin earning the trust of your students and their parents? By letting them know that each and every day you will be there, doing your best to improve their child's education. By showing them with your actions that each child in your classroom will be treated with respect and consideration by you and by others in your room. By never letting go of the idea that drew you to education in the first place—that you can make a difference in the education of today's young people.

A teacher who has been in education for more than ten years explains how trust and respect are still ongoing issues for her:

> I had been having difficulty with a young lady in one of my classes. This was not the first time she had been one of my students, so I was surprised that she was having difficulty with the level of work I expected from her. She seemed to be slacking off, and so I decided to contact her mother before events worsened. Before I could make contact with the mother, however, she called me and began making numerous bitter accusations about the way I was treating her daughter in class. She felt her daughter's inability to do the work was my fault, and she insisted that her daughter was leaving my class at the semester before I could damage her further. The conversation went something like this:
>
> "Thanks to you, my daughter feels like a failure. I know you have it in for her, and I just want to know how we can finish this semester without her flunking your class."
>
> She seemed prepared to begin another diatribe about my failures as a teacher, so I quickly interrupted her before she could get wound up again and said simply, "Well, I must admit, I, too, feel like a failure. I have had your daughter for three classes now, and she has always worked hard for me and scored well above average on all of her work. Obviously, I have lost her this year

for some reason, and believe me, I feel the failure every bit as much as she does. I have done everything I can think of to get her motivated, and I simply cannot seem to reach her. I'm glad you called because I wanted you to know how sorry I am to have lost her. I hope she will have better success in another class."

The silence on the other end of the line was almost deafening. The mother did not know how to respond. I had taken away all of her ammunition by admitting that I, too, was sorry about the way the teacher-student relationship had turned out. Instead of continuing down a road that would lead us both nowhere, we now found ourselves at the same place, sad and disappointed in events rather than people. Instead of feeling offended and threatened by this parent's tone and lack of respect, I chose to offer comfort and a way for the daughter and mother to bring the situation to an end without bitterness. I admit that at first I was offended to have to explain myself to a parent who had previously sung my praises to others in the community; I thought I had already earned her respect and trust. It was then that I realized that respect and trust must be earned continually and that I should never get to the place in my teaching career where I felt that they would be automatically granted based on my past performance.

This is an important lesson for any teacher and one that can help alleviate the feelings of failure that many teachers experience. Teachers will be respected only when they have earned respect, and even then, they must continue to work for the respect of those with whom they come in contact. Respect is never permanent, and the teacher who realizes this will be a much more effective teacher.

If, as a new teacher, you expect to walk into a classroom and immediately have the respect of your students, you are setting yourself up for disappointment and ultimately for teacher burnout.

Another expectation that a quality teacher usually has, and one that is not realistic, is that every student in your classroom wants to learn at the level at which you want to teach. Many students do want to learn, and these students will quickly ascertain that your plan for their education is a solid one. They will do their best to meet your goals, realizing that you are trying to help them be successful in life. Some, however, will not feel this way and simply do not want to be challenged. They simply want to survive the year, get a decent grade, and get on with their lives. They are the most frustrating students ever to walk into a classroom. As a teacher, you know they are capable of better work; you have probably encouraged them, complimented them; basically, you have done everything you know of to motivate these students, and you continue to feel as though you are failing. First of all, never give up on these students. Some of them will eventually come around to your way of thinking and see the bigger picture that you are trying to show them. Some of them, though, never will. You cannot consider this your failure. Many factors have figured into this student's attitude toward education, and you are only one of them. You may be surprised years later when these students contact you and tell you that although you may not have realized it at the time, you were still making a difference in their lives.

A drafting teacher was surprised to receive this e-mail, sixteen years after having this student in his class. The note came from a student who was currently employed as a kitchen designer for a major home improvement company: "I just wanted to say thank you. Tell your students they can be whatever they want if they just pay attention to you . . . if you got through to just one student, it was me. You taught me how to think and act like a man, but still have a sense of humor about life and people. Thank you for all you have done for me in life and in my chosen profession."

As a teacher you will probably never realize how important you were to certain students. You should never feel like a failure because you believe you have lost a student. Many years later you may find that you never really lost him or her at all.

I WANT TO MAKE A DIFFERENCE—NOW!

Most teachers choose to become teachers because they want to make a difference in the lives of young people. They want to leave something positive behind in the world, something that shows that they have made an impact on another person's life. This expectation is a noble one, but gauging your success as a teacher on this concept is a guarantee that, at some point, you will experience teacher burnout. Why? Because in your teaching career, you will experience many, many days when you feel like no one appreciates what you are trying to do. Those students who have come to you and told you what you have taught them and how you have helped them will become a blur in the face of the present where no one seems to care.

Successful teachers, those who experience relatively little burnout, have already learned this lesson, and they realize that for every success they enjoy, they may also have to deal with a few failures. These teachers have come to the realization that expecting constant positive feedback in order to feel good about themselves will put them on the quick track to teacher burnout. If you go into teaching with the idea that you will receive numerous pats on the back and glowing praises for your incredible teaching style, then you are setting yourself up for major disappointments in your teaching career—disappointments that will eventually take all of the pleasure out of teaching for you.

If you are intent on being a good teacher, on teaching your students in the very best way that you can every day that you are in the classroom, then you are already a successful teacher. Some days, everything may seem to go wrong; nothing seems to be working the way you want it to; no one seems to want to listen to a word that you have to say. You must learn to simply say a word or two of thanks at 3:00 when these days finally end and tell yourself that the next day will be a better day.

Teachers, by the very nature of their profession, are somewhat like actors. They get up in front of others and try to sell them on what they are presenting. Unlike actors, however, teachers do not get the standing ovations or critical acclaim; they just keep getting up there on that stage every day, pouring their hearts and souls into something that sometimes no one wants to hear. No wonder they sometimes become discouraged!

Do not become discouraged if it seems that no one notices how hard you are working or how much love you have for education. As a teacher, your expectations should be clear; you are working as hard as you can to teach as much as you can to as many as you can. The satisfaction of knowing your expectations are being met, even if no one seems to notice, makes you a success. Measure your success as a teacher against what you hope to accomplish with your classes. By doing this, you will be making a difference in the lives of your students, and *you* will know it. Let that feeling and nothing else be your motivation and reward.

Take time to enjoy the small victories that will come your way as you work hard teaching your classes. Sometimes, a short letter from a parent letting you know that you are appreciated can go a long way toward giving you the strength to continue doing your best.

Another teacher shares how a simple note, sent at just the right time, gave her the encouragement she so desperately needed:

'I was just finishing up the semester in one of my advanced classes, and things were not going as smoothly as I had expected. Some of the students were become disheartened at the work level, and some even seemed to be downright rebellious. I began to question myself as a teacher. Was I really expecting too much? Did I need to let up? Was I losing my students?

The very last day of class, as I was grading finals and thinking about the next semester, an e-mail popped up on my screen.

"Just wanted you to know how much Jess has enjoyed your class. She talks about the books she has read all of the time. She knows a lot more than I would ever dream of. Whenever she sees a history show on TV regarding what she's studying, she stops and watches it. That has helped me learn more too. Anyway, I think she has learned a lot under your teaching and appreciate the effort you have made to make her a better student and writer. Have a Merry Christmas and may God truly bless you and your family."

That e-mail was all I needed to convince myself that I was still on the right track. I took it as a sign that if I remained true to what I believed, everything would work out.

Enjoy the small victories. You truly are making a difference in your students' lives when you put their education first and foremost in your classroom. Keep the e-mails and notes that you receive, and when you feel like nothing you are doing is worthwhile, take them out, read them, and remember why you chose teaching as your career.

A JURY OF YOUR PEERS?

The final reason teachers become burned out in education has nothing to do with the students, the parents, or even the workload. Incredibly, the final reason comes from an unexpected source—other educators. Principals, superintendents, and other teachers can very easily bring you down in your efforts to become a successful teacher. If you find yourself in a school corporation where everyone is supportive and committed to bringing quality education to the students, stay there. No amount of money can buy this type of atmosphere.

Unfortunately, some in the educational field will not encourage you as you attempt to become a successful teacher; some will actually discourage you, and some may even attempt to discredit your efforts. Your decision to be a serious and committed educator makes them uneasy. This is when the most serious form of teacher burnout occurs, and this is definitely the most difficult to overcome.

If you are teaching in a school system that has a principal who is primarily dedicated to providing a quality education to all of the students in your school, and one who is willing to challenge his teachers to do the same, then you are in an exceptional environment. Many principals can voice the sentiment, but few are willing to actually confront the issues that keep education from being the number one priority. What are these issues and how can they cause teacher burnout?

A teacher who taught for forty years makes this troubling assessment:

As I look back now on my first five years of teaching, I realize how ill prepared I was to teach or coach. I believe that in the early years a teacher teaches like he was taught and coaches like he was coached. My high school and college teachers and coaches stressed the fundamentals, were very disciplined, and cared about young people. Oddly enough, it was only when I went to graduate school that I came in contact with teachers who didn't seem to really care about their students and who viewed their assignment as doing research and going to conventions and conferences so they could be recognized by their peers and rewarded by their administration. Since then, I have taught with teachers who hated what they were doing and couldn't wait for early retirement. I can honestly say that I never got up in the morning and said, 'I don't want to go to school today.'

As a new teacher, you will, unfortunately, meet more teachers who have given up on teaching than who are dedicated to providing educational opportunities to their students. They will view your enthusiasm with detached cynicism, certain that you will not be able to maintain your standards. These are the teachers who pass out a stack of worksheets at the beginning of class almost every day and retire behind a newspaper or who pop in the latest movie to keep their classes entertained. These are the teachers who take as many days as they possibly can to attend whatever they can; they would rather do anything besides actually face their students every day and teach them what they need. You are a threat to them, and they look forward to the day when you join them so that things can get back to normal. These teachers, for some reason, also seem to hold the most power in the hierarchy of teachers in the corporation.

If you have a weak administrator, then your problems are compounded. Few administrators are actually willing to confront a veteran teacher and demand that he or she teach. Why not? Because it's much easier not to rock the tenure boat. Teaching is one of the few careers where after a certain number of years, one is basically guaranteed a position in a school corporation barring an incredible blunder by the teacher. Failure to teach does not apparently qualify.

Lack of professionalism, then, is the number one reason that most good teachers decide to pursue an alternate career. They go into education believing that all teachers want what is best for their students and find that many of their fellow teachers are in education for other reasons. This becomes somewhat disheartening for the new teacher who has always believed that the definition of a fine teacher was directly commensurate with the teacher's actual performance in the classroom.

A first-year teacher from southern Illinois discusses her first view of this type of environment and how she reacted to it:

> As exam week approached, a veteran teacher came to me and told me that she had heard I was going to allow those students who had earned an A in my class for both nine weeks to exempt themselves from the final exam. I teach an advanced class, and the number of students who had earned an A in both terms was minimal. She asked me if I had cleared this with the principal. When I told her that I did not realize I had to, she replied, "Oh, I'll talk to him for you." I later learned that she had actually approached him and hinted that I was doing something against some unwritten school policy. I felt blindsided. I thought that I was in charge of my classroom and that I was making responsible decisions as a teacher. I was not ready for the school politics in this situation, nor had I even sought them out.

Similar stories can be heard from almost any teacher in any school corporation. Another teacher shared this story:

> I had been in a certain school district for only a year or so when the principal approached me and told me that he had a complaint from a student that I was

expecting too much. The student wanted to transfer to another section of the same course because according to him, "They don't have any homework in that section." I thought this sounded ridiculous, but as a new teacher, I did not want to cause any problems so I told the principal that if he wanted to move the student at the semester then I would agree to it. The semester ended in about three weeks, and the student currently had a 13 percent in my class. Imagine my shock when the principal said, "Let's go ahead and move him now so that he can have the opportunity to pass the semester." I couldn't believe I was hearing him correctly, but that's what he said, and that's what he did. The next year the same principal actually started a new section of the class I was teaching simply for those students who didn't want to do the work required for my class. That was when I first realized that education was not always about education. I never got over that feeling of disappointment.

And finally, here is a story that almost every teacher who hears finds hard to believe, but one that actually occurred in a small school district in the Midwest:

I was teaching a dual-credit class where the students in my class were also receiving credit for a nearby college. When the time came to sign up for the class for the next year, thirty-two students signed up for class. I explained to the guidance counselor that the college only allowed twenty-one to be enrolled in the course because it was a writing class, so the decision was made to add an afternoon class for those students who were in vocational programs that met in the morning. All seemed fine until a coworker in my department heard about the schedule. Upset that I would have two classes of fifteen students, she actually called the university and contacted the department to ask if this policy actually existed. I got an e-mail from my mentor at the college asking me what was going on at our school. I was shocked. I could not believe that a fellow teacher would do this. My relationship with this person was never the same; I felt that she had questioned my professionalism.

How can a new teacher protect herself from problems of this magnitude? Three simple strategies can help immensely: (1) Find a professional teacher and create a strong relationship with him or her. (2) Isolate yourself from those individuals who seem to threaten the principles you believe in. (3) Say as little as possible about the problems in your school. The first two are easy to understand and easy to implement. Every school has strong teachers, teachers who believe just like you do and will support you in your attempts to be an educator. Align yourself with these individuals. Eat lunch with them, sit with them at faculty meetings, and stand with them in the halls. In other words, surround yourself with those quality teachers in your school who will be there for you and encourage you. Stay as far away as you can from those teachers who are simply putting their time in; negativity is contagious. The third one is a bit more difficult to explain but just as important. Remember that little corner of your world from chapter 1? You can change your little corner of the world, but you cannot change unprofessional teachers. Discussing them or trying to change things in your school corporation will usually backfire. Stay focused on your own classroom and continue to do your best. Find satisfaction in knowing that you are doing what you need to do, not on wishing that others would also value their students' education.

FOLLOW THE YELLOW BRICK ROAD

Nearly everyone has seen or read the classic *The Wizard of Oz* where Dorothy searches for a way back home, the Scarecrow wants a brain, the Tin Man a heart, and the Lion courage. If the characters stay on the yellow brick road, they know that they will find what they need at the end. They soon realize, however, that the things they were searching for were already within them. How did they realize this? By following the yellow brick road. This story is a perfect metaphor for teaching. The yellow brick road is the path that leads to success in a teaching career, and along that path you will often encounter things that will make you doubt your ability to ever reach your goals. Within you, however, you already have the tools to succeed. You have the desire to share with others your love of education, the courage to stand by your convictions—even among difficult obstacles that threaten your commitment—and the intelligence to discern which parts of education and your environment will keep you going in the right direction. You already know the way; you just have to stick to the path. At the end of the movie, Dorothy realizes "there's no place like home" and vows that if she ever wants to go searching for something, she will never search farther than her own backyard because "if it isn't there, I never lost it to begin with." This, too, can apply to teaching. As long as you stay within the confines of what you truly believe is best, you will never lose your way.

Teacher burnout is not a given. You do not have to experience teacher burnout. Recognizing the signs early, having realistic expectations, surrounding yourself with the right people, and refusing to veer from your path will allow you to reach your goals without burning out on the job that you love.

KIDS SAY THE DARNDEST THINGS

The Experts Speak

What do most of the students in today's schools actually want from their teachers? As a first-year teacher, you may expect to use only one teaching style, one that will work for all of your classes. Different types of students and classes, however, require different types of teachers. Many of the techniques that work well in the elementary and middle schools will not always work in the secondary environment. Whether or not the school tracks its learners, by the time students reach high school, a natural separation usually occurs. High school classes often break up into remedial, general, and advanced or honors classes. The remedial students are those who for various reasons have fallen behind other students and now find themselves in a difficult position. Because of increasing state requirements and additional societal pressures, most schools offer remediation in math, science, and English. General education classes in these areas are, by definition, designed for those students who will go on to technical schools or directly into the workforce. The advanced or honors classes are generally considered by those students who plan to receive an academic honors diploma and attend a four-year college or university. Obviously, not all students fall into these three neat categories, but generally, students in high school follow one of these distinct paths.

The remedial class is certainly one of the most challenging classes for a teacher, regardless of how many years he or she has been teaching. Why? Many of these students have been shuffled throughout the educational system during most of their school years. Some of them were passed through crucial years without learning the necessary skills that would allow them to succeed at the next level. They have become frustrated with schools, teachers, and even their classmates. By the time you enter the picture, they have given up on ever understanding the concepts that their fellow classmates seem to grasp so easily. Discouraged and defeated, many of these students seem to have already decided they will never be anything more than failures.

Many teachers find themselves giving up on these students who have given up on themselves. As a teacher who cares about his or her students' education, you may also find yourself becoming frustrated by the inability of some of your remedial students to achieve even the minimal standards that you or even your state requires.

Surprisingly, these students know exactly what they need, and they will sincerely appreciate the efforts of a teacher who will work with them in order to meet their needs.

Remedial students were asked the following question: What type of teacher do you need in order to feel that you are actually learning something in your class?

Here are the top five answers in order of the answer most frequently given:

1. I need a teacher who will teach me something over and over until I get it, and one who will try to find different ways to teach it to me.
2. I need a teacher who will make me feel confident about myself.
3. I need a teacher who will not give up on me, one who cares.
4. I need a teacher who will not treat me like I am stupid.
5. I need a teacher who acts like she enjoys teaching my class.

This list is heartbreaking to read. Many of the students in your remedial classes do not ever show this side of themselves in the classroom. They may appear sullen, withdrawn, listless, uncaring, and even rebellious. This is their protective shell, and they have worn it for so long that only the most determined teacher will break through.

Consider for a moment what their educational lives have been like. As tests were passed back, they watched as their classmates received As and Bs, only to be handed one more F, clearly visible to all in red ink. Whenever a teacher called on them in class, they either met the question with a blank look, or later, a sarcastic remark. They were labeled failures long ago, and the type of teacher they need is definitely not the same type of teacher who faces a roomful of overachievers competing for an A.

One young student wrote at the bottom of this questionnaire, "No one ever asked me before what I needed in a teacher. I always felt like whatever teacher I had didn't really care if I learned or not. I don't want to fail. I want to pass. Thanks for asking me."

If we want to make a difference in education, this is our main challenge. We must find teachers who will teach the students that are the most difficult to teach. We can never allow ourselves to give up on these young people. The educational buck of failure must stop here—in your room. These are the students that need to know every single day how important their education is to you.

The students in your general education classes, on the other hand, will perhaps be the biggest challenge you face as a teacher. The students in the remedial class will challenge you because they seem so far behind, and you may feel that you lack the training to catch them up in your class. The general education student, however, can be an even more difficult challenge. Why? Many of our general education students have become perfectly content to be mediocre. They feel much smarter than those students in the remedial classes; they know they have sufficient skills to survive in the "real world," and many of them have absolutely no desire to be challenged in the classroom. Obviously, some students in the general education classes have respect for education and understand exactly how much knowledge they will need in order to be successful at the next level. These students, unfortunately, are the exceptions. Perhaps nothing will emphasize this point better than the top five answers general education students gave when they were asked this question: What three qualities do you think a teacher should have in order to be successful in his or her occupation? Their answers were quite different from the remedial students' answers, yet in their own way, they were just as tragic. These, too, are listed in order, beginning with the answer given most frequently.

1. A successful teacher has a good sense of humor and is fun to be around.
2. A successful teacher is nice to the students.
3. A successful teacher is a friend to all the students.
4. A successful teacher is one who treats all students fairly and doesn't have favorites.
5. A successful teacher is one who listens to the students.

All of these traits are certainly commendable ones for a teacher to have, but the question must be asked, do these qualities in a teacher actually allow students to learn at a higher rate? Are these truly the qualities of a successful teacher? When asked, the remedial students concentrated on teaching methods when they discussed a teacher's effectiveness, whereas the general education students focused mainly on personality. What does this mean and how can you apply this to teaching?

Some general education students merely want to be entertained, and they fill their schedules with the easiest electives and minimum requirements for graduation. Most of them feel that they are already qualified to enter the workforce or to pursue the career choices they have made. School has nothing left to teach them. With today's vocational programs, students are often excited and enthusiastic about their futures and see absolutely no reason to continue to study English, math, or science when they could be strengthening their skills in welding, auto mechanics, or computer-aided drafting.

Vocational and other work programs offer excellent opportunities for high school students, and teachers should not be surprised when students would rather be attending these programs than reading *Macbeth* or dissecting a frog. This is why the challenge for these teachers is perhaps the greatest challenge of all. How do you convince a student who may end up earning more than you before he is twenty years old that he needs to learn what you have to teach him?

This is where your enthusiasm and sheer love of teaching can be infectious. When your students understand that you love what you are doing and that you cannot wait to share it with them, most of them will respond in a positive way. Have something new for them to learn every single day and try to show them ways that they can immediately apply the knowledge they are gaining. Do not allow them to do mediocre work; prepare them for a world that will demand much more from them. By doing this, you will be teaching them to be successful long after they leave high school. Unfortunately, this is where you may also have to teach them another lesson that they will soon learn in the workforce—accountability. Students need to pass your class in order to graduate, and if necessary, you must be prepared to teach them the lesson of failure. Teaching general education students most certainly can provide a challenge for a new teacher, but once again, word will eventually get around in your school that you are a teacher who has high expectations for her students, no matter which students she is teaching. After that first year, students will come to your classroom already knowing that you have a commitment to their education.

Advanced or honors classes are obviously the most interesting classes for many teachers. These students have already mastered the basics, yet they realize that they require much more than just the basics in order to succeed at a collegiate level. They demand as much, if not more, from their teachers than they sometimes demand from themselves. Many teachers enjoy these classes the most because they themselves are often challenged by the work and by the students. Academic students responded to the question about what type of teacher was the most effective in a completely different way from the first two groups. Clearly, these students see their teachers as capable of opening many doors for them. Again, the most frequent response is listed first.

1. The teacher who most impacted my education was the one who challenged me to perform at a high level and would not let me settle for doing less than the best that I could.

2. The teacher who most impacted my education was the one who seemed to honestly care about my future and attempted to prepare me to succeed in college.

3. The teacher who most impacted my education was the one who was passionate about the subject that was being taught and attempted to share that passion with us.

4. The teacher who most impacted my education was the one that required me to work hard for the grades that I received, giving me a sense of accomplishment when I met his or her standards.

5. The teacher who most impacted my educated never wasted my time. We always had something to learn, and I always felt challenged to learn it.

Another comment that appeared frequently was that the students realized that the teacher was committed to being a lifelong learner herself. Students recognize and respect those teachers who are still open to learning new ideas or seeing things in a new way.

One student commented, "The day that I explained a literary passage in class and my teacher told me that she had never looked at it that way, and that I had opened her eyes to something new in the novel, was one of the proudest days in my education. From then on, I began reading in a new way, searching for a different or deeper meaning in everything I read. Her simple comment changed how I viewed both the teacher and the class. From then on I had the confidence and desire to explore literature on my own. I wanted to find new and different things in everything I read."

Teaching a student a thirst for knowledge or a skill that he will need in order to succeed in college is exciting; teaching a student to enjoy something for life, however, is the ultimate reward.

The students in the advanced classes were also told that they could write any comments that they wanted to in order to better explain their answers. Here are a few of their comments.

"The most effective teachers enjoy teaching and feel great knowing they are passing on their knowledge to younger individuals who will grow up to use it for bigger and better things. If they don't care to give this 100 percent effort, then why are they teaching? If they're not going to give their best effort to their students who want to learn and absorb knowledge, they should find another profession. I think a teacher has to have heart, a real love for education and passing it on to her students."

Another student wrote this: "Certain teachers try to be liked by all of the students, so they make their classes entirely too easy. All classes should be somewhat challenging to their students. When I took this easy class, I thought to myself, 'What am I doing here?' It was a required class, unfortunately, so I had to take it. I hated every moment of it. I thought it was completely boring and useless because I wasn't learning a single thing. To me school should be about learning, not just having a good time trying to be liked by everyone."

A student taking a combination of general and advanced classes wrote these comments: "Out of all the teachers I have ever had, the ones who made the biggest impact on me are those who put their job first and social life second while in the classroom. So many teachers spend most of our, the students', class time discussing a current event taking place in their lives or what they did over the weekend. Instead of teaching a lesson, most teachers sit at their desk and have an in-class discussion over everything except anything related to the class. Why are these people in teaching?"

These words are from a student who sees things differently from some of her peers: "Everyone told me I would like this teacher. I thought she was nice, but I quickly found out things I definitely did not like. All she seems to care about is what students think of her. She wants to be cool and easy. I sit in her class bored because the work isn't challenging. I never listen, and I have an A. People who normally receive Ds receive As, not because she teaches well, but because she's easy. This is a required class, or I would drop it at the semester. I have not learned one single thing from her class, and I am worried that I will do poorly in this area in college because of it. I want a teacher who makes his/her students think."

And a final comment from a student who decided to form her own opinion about a teacher: "This year I was introduced to a teacher that I had heard horrible things about. People told me she was hard and above all would hate me. I was scared to take this class, but I was looking at the big picture and that was college. I later learned just how wrong people were about her. She is the best teacher I have ever had. She pushes and challenges her students to be the best they can be. Although she is tough, when a student receives a good grade, he or she feels a sense of accomplishment. I hope I meet more teachers as hardworking as she is."

Most of the students who are taking advanced academic or honors classes truly want to improve their minds as well as improve their chances for reaching their goals.

As a teacher, the many different types of students and classes that you teach may, at first, overwhelm you. Keeping in mind exactly what type of teacher is needed for the different types of students will help you maintain your focus and, in addition, will help you become the teacher that you want to be.

I GET BY WITH
A LITTLE HELP
FROM MY FRIENDS

Personal Relationships at School

You've attended your first staff meeting and been introduced to many of your colleagues as well as administrators, secretaries, custodians, and teacher aides. How will you fit in with these groups? What, exactly, should your relationship be with each group?

Where do you go with your questions? This chapter serves as a guide to help you create and maintain positive working relationships with those in your school and to introduce you to the types of people that can help you as you begin your own personal quest for excellence in education.

DON'T OVERLOOK WHO'S
RIGHT IN FRONT OF YOU

As you looked around your room on that first day, you probably noticed how clean and neat everything was. Someone has tried very hard to make your room look nice, and this someone is usually taken for granted by many teachers. School custodians and maintenance workers have an unending job, and one that receives very little attention or praise.

Shortly after school ends for the day, the custodians begin cleaning up the messes that have occurred during schooltime. As a teacher, you can assist them in many ways. Not only will they appreciate your thoughtfulness, but they will also find ways to show you their appreciation. During the last class of the day, try to remember to ask your students to help you pick up the room a bit. Not only does this help the custodians, but it also teaches your students to be considerate of those who take care of them. By the end of the day, there are usually scraps of paper lying about, desks are sometimes askew, small things that take only a few seconds for students to rectify, but can carve minutes off the time the custodian has to spend in your room.

The custodian in charge of your room will definitely notice that you do this, and when the time comes that you need this person to do something for you, he or she will remember your constant thoughtfulness and will reward you with his or her prompt attention to your need. If possible, take the time to get to know the people who take care of your room. If an opportunity presents itself for you to ask your custodian about his or her life, take the time to do so. Get to know this important person in your life as an individual, not just as a person doing a job, remember to give them a thank you note or some kind of treat at Winter Break and at the end of the year.

MAY I TAKE A MESSAGE?

The secretaries in your school have a difficult job. Usually, they have at least six different problems or situations that they are attempting to address at any given moment. Spend just ten minutes observing one of them in the office sometime. You will soon see that they are being inundated with questions and concerns from at least three different people at any one time.

Before you interrupt one of the secretaries in your school, always ask, "Is this a good time to ask you something?" The last thing you ever want to do is to give them one more situation to think about when they are already on overload.

Make sure you understand clearly what your school's secretaries' responsibilities are. Never ask them to do something for you that you should be doing for yourself. One of the most frequent complaints that most school secretaries have is that they sometimes feel that they are taken advantage of. The secretary of your school is not your personal secretary, nor is she your personal whipping post. Often, secretaries are treated to the tirades of teachers simply because they happen to be there at the moment or because they have given a teacher a message from a parent, other teacher, or administrator. The secretary in your school needs you to understand her sometimes-difficult position. Often when teacher-principal, teacher-teacher, or teacher-parent conflicts arise, the secretary may feel trapped in the middle. Never ask her to choose sides. Show her your appreciation occasionally with a thank you card or a plate of treats. The secretaries in your school are usually some of the people who make your day run much more smoothly. Never take them for granted or ask them to do things for you that are not in their job description.

COMRADE-IN-ARMS

The relationships you have with other teachers in the building can become solid, lasting friendships or they can become a battle waiting to become a war. Some teaching staffs are close and supportive professionals, while others prefer to remain in distinct groups. Regardless of the type of staff you have joined, you need to be aware of three things.

1. Never discuss another teacher with anyone—not with students, other teachers, or members of the community.

    Even though your remark may have been harmless, by the time it is repeated to the teacher, it will have lost its original interpretation. Unfortunately, some people (especially students) enjoy causing trouble between teachers. Although you may think the students will respect your confidences, they will not. Many teaching relationships that could have been advantageous to both parties have become strained beyond repair by seemingly innocuous remarks that become exaggerated. Students are not the only guilty parties in this area. Sometimes other teachers and even administrators seem to enjoy stirring up members of the faculty.

    A teacher recently gave the perfect example of this.

    It was close to Christmas Break and the students as well as the teachers were getting restless. At our school we have a policy that the principal has asked us to follow that states that teachers may wear jeans to school on the Fridays that are paydays. Teachers pay a dollar to the scholarship fund in order to wear jeans to school on these days. Well, a few days before break, I couldn't help noticing how many teachers were wearing jeans to school. I admit, I was a little envious at their nerve, but I couldn't seem to bring myself to go against what our principal had asked of us in this regard. I happened to notice that another teacher was more dressed up than usual on one of these days, so I walked up to her and said, "Well, you look very professional today." She replied by saying, "Why, is someone wearing jeans today? I hadn't noticed." I smiled and said, "Well, I've seen a few pairs of jeans this week." This was at lunchtime. Between classes near the end of the day, some of my students came up to me and said, "Our teacher last hour said that you said she wasn't a professional because she was wearing jeans today." I didn't know what to say to them. I felt like the person who had been unprofessional. Simply by making a casual remark to a fellow teacher, I had become the judge and jury of another teacher. I felt terrible about it.

Ask any teacher and he or she will tell you a personal example of how something that was said to another person about a teacher created a tremendous conflict. Be very aware of everything you say to your students, fellow teachers, or anyone about another teacher, student, or administrator. Your mother was correct when she repeatedly warned you, "If you can't say anything nice, don't say anything at all."

2. Support the decisions of other teachers in your school, even if you do not agree.

Sometimes this is a very difficult thing to do. Support, however, is not the same as agreement. Every teacher has the right to teach her class and make decisions based on what her values are. Each of us is entitled to learn from our mistakes in our own way. By supporting your fellow teachers, you open a line of communication that can establish a learning environment for all. Be there for your fellow teachers when you see that they are struggling. Offer to help in any way you can.

3. Try to create and maintain positive relationships with the teachers in your school.

Perhaps the only thing you have in common with any of them is the fact that you teach in the same place. If you have joined a faculty where the teachers get together outside of school and socialize periodically, then consider this a definite plus. If they do not, perhaps you could begin this with the other new teachers that were hired with you. You will find that there are many benefits to spending time with your colleagues in an informal setting.

LET YOUR COUNSELOR BE YOUR GUIDE

One resource that is available to you, and one that many new teachers fail to utilize, is the guidance counselor. Small schools may have only one or two counselors and larger schools may have many, but they all have one thing in common. They are a source of information for a new teacher. Get to know the guidance counselors in your school as soon as you can. Why? Quite simply, they usually know the students better than any other resource person in the school.

As a teacher, you may notice a student who seems to be going through a rough time, or one who is exhibiting major personality changes. Make sure you mention this student to your counselor and suggest that he make an appointment to check in with the student. Part of your job is to be aware of problems your students may have and to refer them to someone who can help. Don't try to decide yourself if a student needs counseling, and you should never attempt to do serious counseling with a student yourself. Watching a few episodes of Dr. Phil does not give you the training or the resources that your school counselor has. Legally, you could be opening yourself up to some serious problems by walking the very fine line between teacher and counselor.

A FINAL THOUGHT

As you begin your first year of teaching, you will encounter many different types of people. Smile at them all, don't be afraid to ask questions, and above all, reserve judgment about them, at least until Winter Break.

IT'S THE "PRINCIPAL" OF THE THING

Remember when you interviewed for the job? Remember how the principal seemed so approachable and caring? Well, he may still be that way, but there are basically three things he wants from his teachers.

1. Handle your own discipline. Although this may be difficult as a first-year teacher, you need to know exactly what kind of atmosphere you want in your classroom, and then you need to find a way to make that happen. If you are really struggling, find a teacher who is known for getting results and confide in him or her. Most teachers are more than willing to pass on what has worked and what has not worked. Often, a first-year teacher will be quick to send problems to the office, mistakenly thinking that by sending her discipline problems there, the principal will believe she is staying on top of things. Try to handle as much of your own discipline as you can. Don't go running to that "approachable" principal or assistant principal who is already buried in paperwork.

2. Keep your students busy and working on task. Make sure that you are prepared to fill the entire period with a variety of worthwhile learning experiences. If the principal or assistant principal walks by your room fifteen minutes before class is over and your students are talking or sleeping, your lack of preparation will be noted.

3. Get involved. Try to attend at least one sporting event or other extracurricular event a month. Even if you are coaching another sport, try to attend other activities when you can. This may only require an hour or two of your time per week, but the benefits of this have already been discussed, and your principal will notice that you are there. Not only will he or she appreciate your support, but in many circumstances, your help could also be beneficial. Volunteer to help whenever you can. When you do attend functions at school, be alert to areas where you can assist visitors, students, or parents.

The above suggestions come strictly from those who are teachers and have worked with principals in many different types of schools around the country. Mr. Kirk Booe, the principal at Covington High School in Covington, Indiana, is much more precise about what he truly needs from his teachers.

Mr. Booe received his license in administration after completing his graduate work at Indiana State University. He was a teacher, coach, assistant athletic director, and assistant principal before joining the staff at Covington. This is one of the reasons for his success as a principal. He has been in many different positions of authority and can understand the problems that may occur in each of them. The following qualities are the ones that he looks for and admires in his teachers:

One of the first qualities I look for is professionalism, and this encompasses a wide area. I expect my teachers to be prepared to teach their classes at the highest level. As professionals this should be their number one goal. I also expect them to be professional in their behavior. Student-teacher relationships must be kept at a professional level in order for the classroom to run smoothly and education to occur. Teachers are role models, and unfortunately, young people today desperately need positive role models; therefore, a teacher should be an ethical and responsible role model. Finally, I appreciate those teachers who are professional in their appearance. They present themselves to the students and to the community in a way that brings honor to the school. They arrive at school early and stay late. Nothing appears less professional to outsiders or students than to see a teacher hurrying to the building late in the morning or rushing out the door as soon as possible in the afternoon. Professionalism is definitely the most important quality. A teacher who behaves in a professional manner is a credit to the students, faculty, community, and administration.

Another important quality that goes hand in hand with professionalism is responsibility. I do not expect to have to remind my teachers of professional deadlines. Paperwork is a necessary evil in almost every job situation, and I expect promptness without prompting. A teacher's responsibilities do not end in the classroom; I also appreciate those teachers who follow the guidelines and procedures that have been established by the school system. A teacher who follows the rules and enforces the rules consistently provides a safer and more educational environment for our school. Another trait I appreciate is foresight. Those teachers who see what needs to be done and are responsible enough to get the job done without being asked are worth a great deal. A responsible teacher looks at the big picture, not just at how things affect him or her personally.

Along with professionalism and responsibility comes evaluation. The best teachers constantly evaluate their teaching methods. They are not afraid to modify their teaching techniques or to try something new. They look for feedback from students, other teachers, parents, and other professionals in an attempt to strengthen their teaching skills. They are capable evaluators of their students and provide positive reinforcement in order to maximize learning. Quality teachers are constantly learning; they never feel that they have completely mastered teaching but instead are continually looking for ways to improve.

Finally, and although I say this with an attempt at humor, the intent behind it is a serious one. Teachers who excel in teaching understand that there is a time and place for everything, and in most cases, school is not it. They do not let themselves become sidetracked with petty grievances or unimportant issues. They are never critical of another's methods, opinions, or ideas. They focus on what does work instead of dwelling on what does not. They arrive at school each day prepared to teach, and they do their best to leave everything else outside the walls of the school.

When I find a teacher who is like the one described above, or one that has the desire to be like the one described above, then I have a teacher who will accomplish great things.

Mr. Booe's words should give all teachers, not only those who are just starting out in the profession, a measuring stick by which to measure their success.

PASSING ON TO OTHERS WHAT WORKS

Your job as a teacher does not end in the classroom. As you begin teaching, you will find yourself developing your own list of what works and what does not work. You will also find that your list of what qualities you need as a teacher may change as you find yourself adapting to your students' needs in order to educate them in the best way that you can. Another responsibility, then, is to share your successes and failures with others, to take an active role in helping other teachers become more effective educators. Listen, read about, and study those who have become successful teachers; develop your own style based on this knowledge, and in turn, pass it on.

Dr. Kirk Freeman is a former teacher and administrator who now manages his own consulting firm called Discovering Excellence. Dr. Freeman leads workshops and in-services and provides consultation services for teachers, administrators, parents, and community members

Dr. Freeman states that teachers who are the most effective in the classroom usually exhibit these three qualities:

1. A passion for teaching children: For teachers to be truly effective, they must have a passion for what they are doing. They actually enjoy being around young people and providing them with a quality education. That "inner drive" must be a part of their personality. These teachers not only care for children, they also believe that everyone can learn.

2. An educated risk-taker: Teachers must be willing to take educated risks. The need to remain updated and the willingness to try the latest research-based teaching strategies must be a part of their teaching repertoire. The very good teachers are always looking for a way to make learning fun and effective for their students. These teachers also make the learning process relevant for each learner.

3. Good communication skills: In order to be effective in the classroom, teachers must possess excellent communication skills. They must keep the students, administration, and parents informed at all times. Along with verbal and written skills, the good teacher is a very active listener. Teachers must be able to truly hear their students' needs and concerns in order to communicate with them.

Dr. Freeman is an individual who listens to teachers, shares what he knows, and then passes on what works.

Educators who have been in the school systems for many years and are still known for their enthusiasm for education can be another source of information for you. Mr. Scott Mathis, who has been a teacher at Seeger Memorial High School in western Indiana for twenty-five years, shares his thoughts on how to remain effective and enthusiastic about education:

I feel that the most important quality for a successful teacher is to maintain a sense of humor. Don't be afraid to laugh and have fun with the students. In addition, sometimes, it's important to be able to laugh at yourself and the mistakes you make.

An effective teacher also has to be willing and able to discipline students in order to be in control of the classroom. Most students need and want a discipline structure whether they realize it or not. Learning cannot take place in an undisciplined environment.

Finally, a good teacher has to be fair in his or her treatment of all students in all situations. In order to do this, the teacher must remain objective. Don't take things too personally or your idea of fairness will be tainted.

With these three qualities, teachers gain the trust and respect of the students. Without that trust and respect, you have nothing.

Finally, Mr. Keith Cleveland, a guidance director for over twenty-five years, explains how students and their perceptions have changed:

An outstanding teacher has many of the qualities of a great actor: passion, ego, and knowledge. Many people work mundane, routine jobs that can be done well without having a passion for the job. Quality teaching, in the classroom or on the practice field, is not a mundane or routine job. To be good at teaching you must have a passion that commands the attention of students. As a counselor I hear from students what they will not tell their teacher or principal and what I hear from them concerning teachers has changed in the past few years. Ten, fifteen, twenty years ago student's complaints were about teachers that expected too much or made it too difficult to get an A. In the past few years, the students' number one complaint is that they are not being challenged. They hate going to the same class every day, not being challenged and not valuing the grade they get.

A desire to impart your knowledge to others is critical. For lack of a better term, I use the word ego. Teachers are not only on stage, they are also directing the presentation and for the most part they have a captive, if not always enthusiastic, audience. A good teacher not only wants to be on this stage, but also wants to use it to improve the lives of the students.

In the teaching profession, knowledge is more than just knowing your subject. While you must know your subject to be an effective teacher, this knowledge alone does not make you a teacher. Knowing how to impart your knowledge to a wide variety of students makes you a good teacher. The best teachers I know are teachers who realize they have not found the perfect way to teach. No matter how many years they have taught, they continue to try something new to improve their teaching.

Kirk Booe, Kirk Freeman, Scott Mathis, and Keith Cleveland are good examples of the types of people who are available to help you, as a new teacher, form your own theories on how to be successful. Seek these types of people out and learn everything they can teach you. Remember to treat those with whom you work, no matter who they are or what position they hold, with professional courtesy. By doing these things, you will be a much better teacher and coworker.

10

WHAT A DIFFERENCE YOU'VE MADE IN MY LIFE

A Tribute to Teachers

Mr. Bill Boone, who taught for over forty years, made this statement shortly after his retirement: "The last forty years have flown by in a heartbeat. I can honestly say that I never once got up in the morning and said, 'I don't want to go to school today.' Someone once said, 'To love what you do and know that it matters; what could be more fun?' I guess that sums it all up, doesn't it?"

By choosing to become a teacher, you have chosen to open a door, not only for yourself but to countless others. Throughout this book you have been given methods, instructions, directions, advice, but above all, you have, hopefully, been given encouragement. Teachers are desperately needed today, more so than at any other time since the beginning of our country. Teaching is an honorable, selfless career, and the difference a good teacher can make in the lives of her students is immeasurable. Almost all teachers have a story or two that they would love to share or something a student has said or written that they read or think about on those days when it seems as though they are standing alone in their commitment to education. Here are a few of those stories and poems.

Good Teachers
By Rachel Stump

Good teachers
Must always show enthusiasm
With their teaching;
Otherwise, who wants to learn from them?

Good teachers
Must always challenge you
With new and exciting things and
Teach you never to give up on yourself.
They must encourage you to always
Try your hardest even if you are on the verge
Of giving up.

Good teachers
Must teach you new things daily
So you will look forward
To their class.
They must always try just as hard as
They expect their students to try;
Otherwise, why should students try to begin with?

ONE VOICE

Dr. Kirk Freeman shares this touching story:

With my new job as a consultant, I have the privilege of traveling the country and leading workshops on effective teaching, brain-based learning, motivation and performing keynote speeches. One of my recent jobs was leading a workshop for parents in the town in which I had previously been the high school principal. As parents were entering the room, I recognized one particular parent that had not been very pleased with me during my years as an administrator. Her son had been in numerous situations in which he did not make appropriate choices; therefore, I had to end up recommending expulsion for the young man. This particular mother would not speak to me after this situation.

The title of the program I was presenting that evening was "Your Child and Mine," and I started the evening by describing the song "One Voice." I explained the significance that we, as individuals, can have on our young people and the fact that each of us can be the "one voice" that saves the life of a child and enables him to feel good about what he does in life.

After the workshop, the mother waited around to talk to me. I was getting nervous in fear of what she might have to say to me. I noticed that she had tears streaming down her face. She walked over to me and whispered in my ear, "Thank you—you were the one voice to my son. You never gave up on him. Even though you had to recommend him for expulsion, you continued to call and talk with him and truly made him believe in himself."

Wow! These were the best words that I could have heard. The mother went on to share how successful he was as an adult. He was graduating from college and looking forward to a successful future.

We never know when we will be that "one voice" that a child hears, that one voice that makes a difference in his or her life.

Here is a poem written by a student, Ashlie D. Scott:

A Learning Experience

She walked into the classroom,
And I began to dread the day.
English was my worst subject,
I hoped she wouldn't stay
Yet as she began to teach,
I began to understand.
The words all came together,
One day, I raised my hand.
"I never understood English,
No one ever took the time,
To teach me how to learn,
Or teach me how to rhyme.
But you took the time to teach me,
You helped me understand.
Thank you so very much
For making me who I am."

Mr. Ron Colson, who taught high school chemistry for over twenty years, learned what a difference he could make in his high school students' college experience. Mr. Colson thoroughly followed his students' collegiate experiences in chemistry and documented his findings for future classes and for his own personal edification. He recorded the college grades for each of his chemistry students and compared them to the grades they made in his chemistry class. He also asked his former students to bring back copies of the tests that they had taken in college chemistry so that he could supplement his teaching if necessary in order to continually align his curriculum with what colleges were teaching. In addition to this, Mr. Colson contacted Purdue University and requested a breakdown of semester grades in chemistry for all of their students and compared it to the students from his chemistry class who attended Purdue. From the years 1984–1989, Mr. Colson's students beat the Purdue average. While only 33.7 percent of Purdue students received a grade higher than a C, 44.5 percent of Mr. Colson's students received a grade higher than a C. From the years 1966–1991, Mr. Colson kept in contact with his former chemistry students and documented his findings. What an impressive way to illustrate to his current students the relevance of his course!

Going the extra mile is a definite way to make a difference in the lives of your students.

Here is a poem written by another student, Derek Peterson:

> What Students Really Need
> Not a teacher who acts like a friend,
> Who will benefit in the end?
> What really matters down inside,
> Is what you're taught while by their side.
> Days of rest and relaxation,
> Will not matter to our generation
> Three years from now when we're in college,
> Suffering because we lack the knowledge.
>
> Although it's not apparent now,
> We'll soon appreciate teachers that taught us how.
> We hated the studies and overload of work
> From the teachers that were known as "jerks."

We now understand their methods and ways,
And all the knowledge that we gained.

Thank you teachers that taught us how
And under the pressure did not bow.
We succeed in life because of you,
We'll be successful in what we do.
We're glad we overcame the ones
That created a class that fitted only some.
Because now in life we have to decide,
Who really made the difference in our lives?

Mr. Steve Welchans received this student letter:

Mr. Welchans,

I just want to tell you how much I do appreciate you and all you've done. I know it may not seem like it on my tests, but I do learn a lot from you. Also, you have helped me get ready for college. I know everything you have taught me will help me all of my life, especially in my career. I have so much respect for you in every aspect. You know almost everything, and you put up with all our bad grades and all our complaining! I really can't put into words how much you are appreciated by everyone and especially me.

This student poem was left on the desk of a teacher on the last day of school:

I Never Said a Word

You handed back our papers the first week of class.
I stared in shock at the grade, the corrections, and the notes you
    had written.
I thought I could already write.
I never said a word.
I went home and cried.
Then, I went through and made every change you had suggested
Even though I thought you were wrong.
I handed it back in and you gave me ten extra points for my efforts
I never said a word.
I just walked away.

You told us to write about a defining moment in our lives.
I wrote about a teacher who tried to ruin her students' individuality.
I stared in shock at the grade, the corrections, and the notes you
    had written.
I never said a word.
I turned away instead.
One day, I received a letter in the mail asking for permission
To publish one of my assignments, one that you had sent in
    without my knowledge.
I will never forget the excitement I felt as I signed the consent form.
I never said a word, though,
Still stubborn to the end.
Now, at the end of the year, I realize what you have done for me.
My dream of becoming a writer is suddenly within my grasp.
And it's because you refused to let me settle for what was and
    made me see what could be.
So, I decided to say two words.
"Thank you."

INSPIRATIONAL LINES

Finally, many lines have been written about teaching, but these quotations truly emphasize the importance of teaching and the timelessness of the art.

"The best teacher is the one who suggests rather than dogmatizes, and inspires his listener with the wish to teach himself." Edward G. Bulwer-Lytton (1803–1873)

"If you think in terms of a year, plant a seed; if in terms of ten years, plant trees; if in terms of 100 years, teach the people." Confucius (BC 551–479)

"One looks back with appreciation to the brilliant teachers, but with gratitude to those who touched our human feelings. The curriculum is so much necessary raw material, but warmth is the vital element for the growing plant and for the soul of the child." Carl Jung (1875–1961)

"A teacher who is attempting to teach without inspiring the pupil with a desire to learn is hammering on a cold iron." Horace Mann (1796–1859)

"What office is there which involved more responsibility, which requires more qualification, and which ought, therefore to be more honorable, than that of teaching?" Harriet Martineau (1802–1876)

"We must view young people not as empty bottles to be filled, but as candles to be lit." Robert H. Shaffer

"I cannot teach anybody anything; I can only make them think." Socrates (BC 469–399)

"The mediocre teacher tells. The good teacher explains. The superior teacher demonstrates. The great teacher inspires." William A. Ward (1921–1994)

"Teaching is the greatest act of optimism." Colleen Wilcox

Finally, a quotation that every teacher should commit to memory:

"Do not train a child to learn by force or harshness; but direct them to it by what amuses their minds, so that you may be better able to discover with accuracy the peculiar bent of the genius of each." Plato (BC c. 427–c. 347)

Someone once said that a teacher touches a future that he or she may never even see. Teaching is, indeed, a noble profession, and the fact that you have chosen teaching as your career says something special about you and your priorities. Welcome to the world of teaching. May your time in this world be as much of a blessing to you as you are sure to be to your students.

This final poem by high school senior Kayla Grubbs should inspire all who wish to be teachers:

Making a Difference

Teachers fill our minds and the good ones touch our hearts,
But the teacher that does both has done more than just her part.
They reveal the path of knowledge, and they even light the way,
Always keeping us focused and refusing to let us stray.
A teacher's job is never easy, mostly it's just rough,
That's why all the good teachers are referred to as "tough."
Teachers teach us many lessons that we need to know,
And teachers know exactly when students can be on their own.
They send us out to live our dreams, knowing they did their best.
Now we know it's up to us; we have to do the rest.
I want to thank my teachers, who helped me along the way.

CHAPTER 10

I'll be a better person with each and every day.
Thank you to those who reached me and always helped me learn
I know that you'll be proud when it's time to take my turn.
Someday I will make a difference, but how I just don't know.
How can I touch someone's life, or know which path I should go?
Some people become nurses or farmers or preachers,
But I know if I want to make a difference, then I'll become a teacher.

ABOUT THE AUTHOR

Chris Boone Cleveland received her bachelor's and master's degrees from Indiana State University and holds a lifetime teaching license in English education. She has taught English at the middle school, high school, undergraduate, and graduate levels. She currently teaches at Covington High School where her courses include Advanced Placement English 11, Advanced Themes and Genres in Literature, Introduction to Composition and Research, and Basic English. She also teaches a freshman writing course for Vincennes University in Indiana.

Chris resides in Covington, Indiana, with her husband, Keith; daughter, Kayla, 18; and son, Dallas, 14. Her spare time is spent collecting unique copper items, reading historical fiction and Civil War nonfiction, gardening, and traveling.